RAMSES

A Memoir

Also by Theodore Dalrymple from
New English Review Press:

Anything Goes (2011)

Farewell Fear (2012)

Threats of Pain and Ruin (2014)

Out into the Beautiful World (2015)

The Proper Procedure and Other Stories (2017)

Grief anf Other Stories (2018)

*The Terror of Existence: From Ecclesiastes to Theatre of
the Absurd* (with Kenneth Francis) (2018)

Neither Trumpets Nor Violins (2022)
(with Samuel Hix and Kenneth Francis)

RAMSES

A Memoir

THEODORE DALRYMPLE

Published by New English Review Press
a subsidiary of World Encounter Institute
PO Box 158397
Nashville, Tennessee 37215
&
27 Old Gloucester Street
London, England, WC1N 3AX

Cover Art and Design by Kendra Mallock

ISBN: 978-1-943003-70-9

First Edition

NEW ENGLISH REVIEW PRESS
newenglishreview.org

To those who have cherished an affection for a faithful and sagacious dog, I need hardly be at the trouble of explaining the nature or the intensity of the gratification thus derivable. There is something in the unselfish and self-sacrificing love of a brute, which goes directly to the heart of him who has had frequent occasion to test the paltry friendship and gossamer fidelity of mere *Man*.

—Edgar Allan Poe, *The Black Cat*

I sometimes hold it half a sin
To put in words the grief I feel:
For words, like Nature, half reveal
And half conceal the Soul within.

— Alfred, Lord Tennyson, *In Memoriam*

E VERYONE SUPPOSES that his dog is the best dog in the world, but it so happens that Ramses was the best dog in the world—the cleverest, friendliest, most expressive, understanding, amusing dog that ever was, and it was only a happy coincidence that he was ours. We have asked all our friends, and they agree. No dog ever merited memorialisation more than he.

It is now nearly thirteen years since he died—as long as we had him with us—and my wife and I still miss him and talk about him often. At difficult moments, we remark how much easier they would be if he had been still with us to console us. I doubt whether, thirteen years after my death, anyone will talk of me in the same fashion, if anyone talks of me at all.

Ramses was a Yorkshire Terrier, *steel and tan* as his passport described him, and he came to us when he was two. An Egyptian friend of my wife's, who had been living in England, was returning to the Middle East and could not take Ramses with her. She brought her young children to inspect our house (and us) to pronounce on whether it (and we) were of a sufficient standard to offer Ramses a new home. They decided that we were, and I told my wife, who had never had a dog before, and who agreed to take

Ramses only because I had long talked of having a dog, that she would soon be surprised by how deeply she would come to love him.

Indeed, our attachment to him was so strong, so intense, that I feel slightly hesitant, or even ashamed, to describe it. Ramses was only a dog, you might say, which in the literal sense is correct: but what is meant by the word 'only'? That Ramses had no eternal soul, as humans supposedly do? That he was not a self-conscious being, that he was an automaton, albeit an elaborate one, as Descartes would have had us believe? Here I experience what I believe psychologists call *cognitive dissonance*, that uncomfortable state in which one holds two incompatible beliefs in the mind simultaneously without rejecting either, as logic would suggest that we should.

I do not believe in eternal souls (not even in mine, alas), but if someone were to describe Ramses as having been soulless, I should be shocked, horrified, even disgusted, especially if that person had actually met him. And while I do not believe in souls, I also believe that all attempts at a purely naturalistic explanation of human existence, be it Darwinian, Marxist, Freudian or neuroscientific, are doomed to failure, in other words that Man will remain forever a mystery to himself. Alone in the universe, as far as we know, Man is capable of propositional language whose meaning can never be reduced to merely physical terms. Whether I am right or wrong in this is not here the question: the fact is that my philosophical belief is in contradiction to my attitude to, and feelings about, Ramses, with whose soul, if I may so put it, my own was in such close contact. How else can I explain the extraordinary fact that in his presence, I was never unhappy, never bored and never lonely, and that he self-evidently wanted to be with me, or with my wife, at all times? If ever there were soul-mates, we were soul-mates, Ramses, my wife and I.

Here I must confess to something that has worried me ever since Ramses died. Because he always wanted to be with us, we must have caused him repeated unhappiness, for until our retirement three years before his death, we both had to go to work every weekday, leaving him on his own (except for the half-days when the cleaning lady came). He could not have made his misery when we left him clearer had he been possessed of language. He crept low upon the ground and all his movements declined into slow-motion. A single word was sufficient to throw him into the deepest despair: 'Basket!' He knew then that his fate for the day was sealed.

Now that I look back, I wonder whether he knew that we should soon return (soon, that is in human terms, dog-time might be experienced differently, as child-time is experienced differently from adult-time, and twenty-year-old-time from seventy-year-old-time), or whether each day he thought that he was being abandoned forever. If the latter, he experienced hundreds—no, thousands—of abandonments. What unhappiness we must have caused him without wishing to! And this despite the fact that our intended relations with him were those of unequivocal and total benevolence.

He was very good at sensing when we were intending to leave the house, sometimes even seeming to know it before we knew it ourselves. Then he would hide so as to delay being left alone. Our house was quite a large one on three floors, not counting the cellar to which he never descended despite his temperamental curiosity, and there were many places for him in it in which to hide. And here was a strange and impressive thing: he never hid in the same place on two consecutive occasions. It was as if he knew that when he hid before we went out, the first place that we should look for him would be the last place in which we had found him. He would hide under a bed on the top floor and the next time in a cupboard on the first floor. I do not know whether psychologists would count this as having a theory of mind—an understanding of the mental workings or processes of others—but so it seemed to us.

He was so good at hiding that it was sometimes quite difficult to find him and extract him from his hiding place. Once some friends arrived at the house to go out with us to dinner. Ramses sensed that he was soon to be left on his own, so he hid. We couldn't find him even after fifteen minutes of searching, so knowing that he responded to the telephone by barking when it rang, we called our number from a mobile telephone. This had the desired effect: Ramses rushed out from his hiding place on the top floor, barking furiously. He saw us waiting for him and realised at once that he had made a terrible mistake. He immediately applied his brakes, as in a cartoon film, but it was too late, for we now knew where he was. I should add that we had to capture him, because our alarm system with its movement detectors meant that he had to be confined to the hallway while the alarm was on. This was quite a large space, but Ramses didn't like to be confined to it. Between the front door and the hallway was a second door with a stained glass panel through which we were able to watch him, as we left, go round the hallway to test that all the doors to it had been firmly closed.

The next night, as it happened, we went out again to dinner with friends, and the scene was replayed, with Ramses hiding in a different place. We tried the telephone trick again, but this time it didn't work: Ramses was very quick on the uptake and had learned to distinguish a real telephone call from one intended merely to lure him into revealing where he was. He never fell for the trick again, though we tried it several times, even after intervals.

Ramses' misery when we left was equalled only by his joy when we returned. No doubt I could be accused of anthropomorphism for employing such words as joy and misery in connection with a dog, but it seems to me the natural way to speak of Ramses' reactions, and any other way would be forced and no more accurate. He had a special bark when we returned, slightly higher-pitched than usual; when I was in the house alone with him, I could tell from his bark when my wife was about to enter the house, and even when her car arrived in the driveway, for he knew the difference between her car and any other with complete accuracy. Lying half-asleep, he would first prick up his ears and then show unmistakable signs of pleasurable excitement. When he heard her key in the door, his excitement grew to fever pitch, and as she entered, he would jump up and down until she picked him up and cuddled him. It was impossible not to see this as an expression of disinterested love, as there was no reward for it other than an expression of love in return.

These accesses of joy would, presumably, have been impossible without their opposite, the depths of misery occasioned by our departure. Whether the one was worth the other is a question not susceptible to a definitive answer. Those who favour a life full of incident and drama would no doubt say yes; those who favour a quiet life lived on an even keel would no doubt say no. We could not canvass Ramses' opinion on the matter, though I now suspect that he would have preferred to live without these emotional highs and lows.

There was one reunion with Ramses after an absence of a week at a conference that sticks in my memory as both joyful and painful. My wife had not accompanied me, and on my return I re-joined her and Ramses at a friend's house. It was a beautiful day in June, one of those days under an English heaven, and my friend's house had a very large garden with an extensive lawn of at least two acres. On catching sight or sound or scent of me, Ramses fairly flew across the lawn and jumped into my arms, wriggling with joy and frantically trying to lick my face. Again, it was impossible for me not to interpret this as love, for there was certainly no reward for Ramses, such as food, that would have satisfied a behaviourist for whom all behaviour is merely a matter of stimulus, response and reinforcement. It would take mental contortions, in fact, not to describe it as love.

My reunion with Ramses was for me a lovely moment, but as Keats says:

… in the very temple of Delight
Veil'd melancholy has her sovran shrine…

and in that joyful moment, I simultaneously apprehended the inevitable decay of joy brought about by Time. Therefore, in the midst of joy, I was in sadness, happy for the most obvious reason but sad not only because I knew that the moment of joy could not last but that its fleetingness was a reminder of mortality, that Ramses was destined—statistically-speaking, that is—to die before us, though of course he did not know it. He was lucky enough to be able to live completely in the moment, a gift that was quite beyond me. The inevitable decline of pleasure or joy into its opposite, pain, which eventually must preponderate, is the basic pessimistic apprehension of Buddhism, to which the only solution is a kind of indifferent equanimity of which I, at any rate, am incapable.

Another moment of enormous joy—with, of course, the accompanying pain that the joy could not last—occurred when we took Ramses to the seaside for the first time. It was in Wales, Aberdaron to be precise. After her retirement from her hospital, my wife continued to work part of the year as a replacement doctor, and we were spending three months in a village near Bangor in North Wales. One weekend we decided to visit the Llyn Peninsula, the northern arm of Cardigan Bay, making for Aberdaron because it was the last parish before his retirement of the poet-vicar, R.S. Thomas, both in whose poetry and character we had become interested.

Real estate agents use the word *stunning* with promiscuous dishonesty when describing perfectly ordinary properties, as if the sight of a bathroom could stun anyone except, perhaps, a Bushman of the Kalahari; but our first view from the top of the peninsula to the bay below was indeed such as to cause us to halt and draw deep breath.

Aberdaron has a thirteenth-century church only slightly above sea level and a cemetery that that extends up the slope behind it. Its tombstones are of sober black Welsh slate, many of them of drowned sailors or of passengers of early steam packets. They are inscribed—those of them that we were able to read, many being in Welsh—with restrained eloquence, that is to say eloquence for those with a little imagination, the elegantly-carved lettering as fresh after nearly two centuries as the day it was carved. It was here, and how, I should like to be buried, insofar as I should like to be buried at all, though by that stage quite unable to appreciate either the view or the soothing rhythmic susurration of the sea beating on the shore, in a good imitation of eternity. And it was from here that we had the idea of a Welsh slate tombstone for Ramses when he died.

We had the entire beach to ourselves—Ramses, my

wife and I. As soon as he arrived on the beach, Ramses sniffed the air and ran off, mad with joy. Although he was by then twelve or thirteen, old for a dog, he behaved like a puppy. He didn't just run, he leapt. Every hundred yards or so, he stopped to look back and check that we were following him, waiting for us nearly to catch up before running on again, and so on until we reached the end of the beach. He then repeated the performance in the reverse direction. The sea air had an intoxicating effect on him, almost like that of a stimulant drug but without the latter's deleterious effect, a real elixir. The sea air and watching Ramses reinvigorated us too.

We sat on a rock to have lunch. Ramses liked sandwiches: in fact, he liked anything that we ate. It was as if we were tasters for him, or critics. What was good enough for us was good enough for him. He was not a greedy dog, though, far from it. He would eat what he needed and then stop, however much remained in his bowl. Often, he would not eat until we sat down to eat: for him, unlike for so many people nowadays, especially in Britain, eating was for preference a social activity. When we left the house for the evening, we would leave food for him, which he would leave untouched until we returned, when he ate it with appetite.

I used to think of Ramses' moderation in the matter of appetite as a sign of good character, of self-control, but then (alas) it occurred to me that if so, his good character was genetic in origin, for you never see a fat Yorkshire Terrier, unlike fat retrievers and Labradors. The most obvious explanation for this curious distinction is that there is a genetic difference in the breeds. This might not be the whole of the explanation, for I have noticed that fat people tend to have fat dogs, as in paintings by Botero. Therefore, you can have a propensity to obesity without becoming obese, especially if, as in the case of human beings, you are blessed, or cursed, with the gifts of freewill and self-consciousness.

Once we had finished our sandwiches, we settled down to read out loud some of Thomas' poems. Ramses listened with rapt attention. I won't go quite so far as to say that he understood what he listened to; rather his attention was but an example of his intense concentration on us as the centre of his being. Nothing human is alien to me, said Terence, the Roman playwright; Ramses might have said, had he been able to speak, that nothing we did was unimportant to him.

And so we read *The Island*, Thomas' furious denunciation of the God he supposedly served, a curious poem for a clergyman to have written, disapproving as it was of the conduct of the supposedly benevolent founder of the Universe:

> And God said, I will build a church here
> And cause the people to worship me,
> And afflict them with poverty and sickness
> In return for centuries of hard work
> And patience.

Thomas makes reference, surely, to some of the tombstones of the drowned in the churchyard when he writes:

> … and I will choose the best
> Of them to be thrown back into the sea.

Did Thomas' parishioners, few enough, read their vicar's act of accusation against God in whose worship he was leading them? All the photographs of him that I have seen, even those of him when he was young, show him as granite-faced, if not as downright angry, as if everything, Man and the world, were a bitter disappointment to him. If only he had met Ramses, perhaps his stance towards the world would have softened.

Another poet, Christopher Smart, saw not only the benevolence of God in a creature (that is to say, in what Poe called a brute) but a grateful awareness of the beauty of creation by his cat, Jeoffrey:

> For he purrs in thankfulness, when God tells him he's a good Cat.
> For he is an instrument for the children to learn benevolence upon.
> For every house is incomplete without him and a blessing is lacking in the spirit.

If this is all true of a mere cat, think of the blessing of a dog, and not just any dog, but Ramses!

We left Aberdaron with reluctance to return to Bangor, but Ramses' first day on the beach will remain with us always. And when, fourteen years later, my wife suggested that we go away for a few days on the occasion of my seventieth birthday, that she would pay, and that I could choose anywhere I liked, it was Aberdaron that I chose, not only for its beauty, but of course for the now bittersweet memory of Ramses there. This state of melancholy, which is pleasurable and painful in the way that pressing on an inflamed part is pleasurable and painful, is, as Keats puts it:

> … seen of none save him whose strenuous tongue
> Can burst Joy's grape against his palate fine…

And ever since we went to Aberdaron with Ramses, I have

watched people play on the beach with their dogs—in Jersey, Tenby, Brittany—with a mixture of pleasure and envy.

A friend of mine, a distinguished author, once said to me that the mutual love of dog and man is one of humanity's most redeeming features, if not actually the best thing that can be said of it; and it is true that, as one observes the innocent pleasure of a man on a beach with a dog, a pleasure that I once shared but is now lost to me, which is born of undiluted benevolence, one can almost believe in Rousseau's view that Man is born with original virtue rather than original sin. I can for hours watch people play with their dogs on a beach, for example, when they throw a stick for a dog to retrieve. One cannot think ill of a man when he plays on a beach with his dog.

Pascal said that the problems of the world arose from the inability of people to sit quietly in a room on their own; perhaps the same could be said of an inability to play happily with a dog.

It is always difficult to bring a game with a dog to a close. Once (after Ramses' death), we were in the beautiful village of Banne in the Ardèche, near to our house that 'depends on', as the French say, that commune. It was the hour of the siesta; all the shutters were closed and the village was deserted. There was a black and white mongrel, mostly sheepdog, in the square before the church. He had a rather battle-scarred and squashed football with him, and when he saw us, he nudged the ball towards us with his muzzle. It was obviously an invitation to a game, and I kicked the ball gently for him to retrieve. We were still playing the game an hour later, and though it was very simple and I count myself an intellectual, I was not in the slightest bored with it and tore myself away only with reluctance, telling myself that I had more important things to do, though I wasn't sure what. I never saw the dog again, though I looked out for him whenever I returned to the village, but I was pleased to think that I must have reinforced his high opinion of humanity.

Ramses liked to play, but not this particular game. His favourite toy was a rubber rat on the end of a long elastic string. When it bounced up and down (we being the puppet-masters, of course), he would try to catch it in mid-air. It is said that Yorkshire Terriers were bred to catch rats, and once again I found myself thinking—casually, not deeply—about the genetic foundations of behaviour. Such thoughts added nothing whatever to the pleasure of the game, rather the reverse: we murder to dissect.

But Ramses' favourite game was played on the bed. One of us would slam our forearm down on the quilt and Ramses, growling, would pounce on it and hold it between his teeth. He never hurt us, not even when our arms were bare, for he never clamped his jaws to the maximum of their strength: this was virtual hunting, not the real thing. And oddly enough, it was he, not we, who decided when to start and finish the game. He would issue a growl—again, a virtual, not a real one—to indicate the beginning of the game, and when he lost interest, he would simply stop and could not be induced to start again.

I was very pleased that it was he who decided the start and finish of the game, because I wanted him to have a mind of his own and not to be the canine equivalent of a yes-man, that is to say a yes-dog. Of course, most of the major decisions in his life were taken by us, but he had to have a margin of choice if he were to be a companion rather than a slave. There are some people who want the most complete domination over other beings, including human beings, but the price to pay for this is permanent loneliness.

Ramses sometimes showed his independence of mind

on our evening walks together. We lived opposite a rather splendid Victorian Gothic church in the middle of a square, or rather an oval, with a lawn round it and bushes near to it. Almost every night, we walked in a clockwise direction round it twice before returning home. It was a routine, and as I discovered somewhat late in life, there is comfort in routine. Perhaps it encourages or creates the illusion that time has stopped and that nothing will change, which is a comforting illusion when you are as happy as were we. Sometimes, though, for no apparent reason, he would insist on walking counterclockwise, and though I was easily able to impose my will on him, I let him impose his on me.

Once on these evening walks, he became something of a local hero. Not far from our road were several hotels patronised mainly by what used to be called commercial travellers. This created a market for cheap prostitutes, and a demand eventually calls forth its supply. Some pimp, or syndicate of pimps, had the idea of bussing in every weekday evening a team of prostitutes from a nearby town of ill repute. Our road was perfect, from the pimp's point of view. It was quiet, not brightly lit, unfrequented and not much used, or at all, by through traffic. The girls, who were mostly well on in their thirties, stood under the street lamps as if waiting to be drawn by George Grosz in Weimar Berlin. They wore flimsy but gaudy dresses whatever the temperature and were heavily made-up. They were of that cadaverous thinness brought about by a diet of cocaine and cigarettes.

Their encounters with the clients must have been quick to fleeting, the scratching of a physiological itch on the latter's part, and without the slightest pretence of romance that sometimes disguises or softens a little the nature of the transaction. Once the pattern of the trade was established, a white van furnished by the municipality performed a circuit delivering coffee and condoms to the prostitutes in a campaign of what was known as harm reduction. In the morning, we would find used municipal condoms in the gutter or hanging like Ophelia's weedy trophies from the rose bushes in our gardens, thus transferring the risk of catching something from the prostitutes and their clients to the householders as they cleared up the mess.

Two doors from us lived the redoubtable Beryl, a retired research scientist and university lecturer, who did not accept the situation as if it were of geologic inevitability. She went to war against the pimps, a war which lasted a few months but from which she emerged victorious. Her strategy was two-pronged. She arranged a local vigilante group which patrolled the road at night and took down the registration numbers of a kerb crawler's car, intimidating enough in itself, but accompanied by a threat to write a letter next time to the registered owner's address to discourage his return. (I was excused from duty on this vigilante group, because it was known that I was on medical duty one night in three or four for the large prison a mile and a half away.) One evening, the pimp, or one of the pimps, tried to warn Beryl off. He sat in his car, and when she approached him, took out his gun to threaten her. Beryl was not impressed.

'Don't be ridiculous,' said the redoubtable Beryl. 'Put that thing away.' And he did, never to return to the scene of his humiliation.

Beryl's other enemy was the police, but she defeated them too. She went to the local police station to complain of what was happening in our road, previously a tranquil and rather beautiful one. The local inspector said that he did not propose to do anything about it because, as he put it, the girls were unfortunate enough already, coming as they did from bad backgrounds (something which he assumed *a priori*), without also being harassed by the police. Beryl fixed him with her steely eye, no doubt very practised in the upbraiding of unsatisfactory students, and said, with commendable concision, 'That is not the law.'

The inspector gave way, as does any bureaucrat confronted by a determined and potentially dangerous opponent, and ordered his men to clear the street, which they did. The girls were merely moved on to other streets, of course, presumably to ones where there was no Beryl. Thus in the end, both Beryl and the police got what they wanted, Beryl a street without prostitutes and the police a quiet life, a completely satisfactory outcome. The case illustrated a fundamental law of bureaucracy, namely that a bureaucrat acts only when not to do so will give him more trouble than acting. The police inspector, all credit to him, had correctly assessed Beryl's character at one encounter, and realised that she was not the type to give up once she had the bit between her teeth.

But to return to Ramses' small part in the defeat of the prostitutes. We, Ramses and I, were out walking round the church one evening, when Ramses started to bark furiously and strain at the leash. Suddenly the bushes parted and out tottered a prostitute who had been hiding in them from a group of vigilantes not far away, waiting for it to depart.

'Oh f…!' she exclaimed as she ran off, not very fast because her high heels were not suitable for quick getaways.

'Give that dog a bone!' shouted one of the vigilantes. They had suspected the prostitute was in the bushes and had wanted to flush her out.

Mostly, however, our evening walks were uneventful. Ramses would pull on the lead in the direction of a smell, and I would follow and watch him. How intense, how all-consuming was his interest in what he was doing! In fact, his interest was intense and all-consuming whatever he did. He was obedient to the injunction in Ecclesiastes:

Whatever thy hand findeth to do, do it with thy might…

However, the continuation of this passage was often uppermost in my mind:

… for there is no work, nor device, nor knowledge, nor wisdom, in the grave wither thou goest.

There was no evening—of about three thousand such evenings—in the course of which I did not reflect, as I saw Ramses so busy with his affairs, on the fact that I knew he was to die and that he did not, and that I would survive him by many years through no desert or merit of my own. It was a painful thought, but I could not rid myself of it.

Did this superior apprehension of reality, or at least of one important feature of reality, constitute an advantage or a disadvantage, a blessing or a curse? Was it better to live unselfconsciously in the moment, or, by taking thought, be able to foresee the denouement of our lives which is death? To this there is no clear or unequivocal answer, except, perhaps, that it is now the one and now the other. Never to be able to live in the moment is never to experience anything as an end in itself, anything that requires no further justification; but always to live in the moment is (at least for humans, presumably dogs have no choice in the matter) to be imprudent, improvident and almost certainly parasitic on others.

Another old saw ran through my mind on my walks with Ramses, the last lines of Thomas Gray's *Ode on a Distant Prospect of Eton College*. Gray, I surmise, was a man of intense but private emotion, perhaps so intense that he thought that any public expression of it would become unmanageable, would overwhelm and destroy him. Espying the children on the playing fields of Eton, he wrote:

To each his suff'rings: all are men
　Condemn'd alike to groan,
The tender for another's pain,
　Th'unfeeling for his own.
Yet ah! why should they know their fate?
Since sorrow never comes too late,
　And happiness too swiftly flies,
Thought would destroy their paradise.
No more; where ignorance is bliss,
　'Tis folly to be wise.

My folly to be wise was an example of what a young philosopher of my acquaintance calls 'overthinking', the modern tendency, particularly of intellectuals and semi-intellectuals, to turn every experience and every phenomenon into the subject of supposedly deep reflection, often to their own discomfiture. The habit, once established, is not easy to break, and is often a matter of pride to him who has it, a further reason to look down on those who simply skate over or slice through life, merely accepting experience as it comes.

I did my best to rid myself of morbid thoughts, resolving to enjoy my time with Ramses all the more, delighting when he suddenly decided, for no reason that I could discover, that he wanted a longer walk than usual. The breaking of routine gave me pleasure, though a pleasure depending on the existence of a routine to break. Ramses would pull on the lead and turn round to look at me not with a defiant, but a determined look. I could, of course, have pulled him in any direction I chose, but I preferred to give in to his whim, thereby equalising our relationship a little.

But what exactly was that relationship? Although you might say that we *owned* Ramses, we certainly did not think of our relationship to him as being similar to that with our plates, say, or our cutlery. Ownership is not, in any case, itself an entirely straightforward concept. Most people would probably think of ownership as the power to dispose of what is owned in any way one wants, but such unlimited power is only one type of ownership and not by any means the most important. I own my house—certainly no one else owns it—but I am not permitted to burn it down if I wish, and because it is old, I am not even permitted to alter it in any radical way, a restriction on my rights of ownership that I accept and even welcome, since it preserves not just my house but all those around it from aesthetic vandalism. Moreover, there are other things that I own—works of art, books that are the only copy in the world—that I have the legal, but not the moral, right to dispose of as I wish. Of those things, I consider myself as much the custodian as the owner in the full sense: it is my duty to pass them on, either by gift, sale or legacy, to someone or some institution that will take the same care of them. Ownership, then, does not confer unlimited rights over what is owned, except over trivial possessions of no intrinsic worth.

Neither could we (or want to) think of ourselves as Ramses' masters. Certainly, we were dominant, my wife and I, and took most of the decisions that affected his life. I have already mentioned that, the single word 'Basket!' produced an instant state of depression in him when we proposed to leave him for a time; he was not fearful, but miserable. By contrast, when we asked 'Are you coming?'

he was immediately transported by joy, jumping for joy in fact. However, we never exercised our power over him for its own sake, merely to show him who was boss, as masters often do. We could not pretend either, except in very special circumstances, that the unhappiness we caused him was for his own good, teaching him a valuable lesson, as masters often pretend. The circumstances dictated our dominance over him, not any will to power.

Of course, for 99.99 per cent of the time, the question of the nature of our relationship did not arise, which was why it was so happy. Everything between us was taken for granted. Happiness in a relationship is like the bloom of a grape: once it is touched, in this case, by thought, it is lost. That is why all the psychology in the world, all the supposed delving into the mind (much of it bogus and of doubtful sincerity), not only fails to alleviate unhappiness but actually increases it.

The happiness brought by dogs is remarkable. You can see it all around you, if you look. I know my local dogs in England. There is Oscar, for example, our next door neighbour's dog, who is their pride and joy. Then there is Alfie, a dog of mixed breed but handsome, jet black with a white star on his chest, who I suspect is the preserver of his companion's will to live. This man, who did a simple but honourable job that he loved, was struck down by a neurological condition that prevented him from doing it (though, slowly and with difficulty, he could still walk). Forced into a retirement that he did not want, he took Alfie as a puppy, who had that wonderful predisposition of many dogs to love everyone he met and to suppose that everyone loved him. It takes persistent cruelty to destroy this predisposition, and fortunately such cruelty is nowadays very rare. (I shall return to the subject briefly later on.) Alfie was the love of this man's life, so much was obvious. He would speak of Alfie's faults and naughtiness, and disparage him, but with love written on his face. He was ashamed to reveal the depth of his feeling.

Besides being his companion, Alfie was his physiotherapist. I suspect that without him, his companion would have sunk into apathy and inactivity, the psychological antechamber of death.

Then there was Minnie, a wire-haired terrier of great age. Oddly enough, Minnie was, despite the name, a dog rather than a bitch. He was taken for a walk twice a day by an old lady who, being of an extremely retiring nature, would talk only of him. However hard you tried, she would never speak of anything else; and, oddly enough, she was disparaging of Minnie too, calling him a trouble and a nuisance.

'He's more trouble than he's worth,' she would say. 'I don't know why I keep him.'

Her face was deadpan, but it wasn't difficult to guess that Minnie was the focus of her whole life, almost her *raison d'être*.[1] And indeed, when the inevitable happened and Minnie, who was seventeen, died, the old lady was very rarely seen again, not even to go about her shopping. One could only imagine the depth of her mourning for him, the devastation of her loss. Is Tennyson right when he says:

I hold it true, whate'er befall;
  I feel it when I sorrow most;
  'Tis better to have loved and lost
    Than never to have loved at all… ?

---

1 In Camus' novel, *The Stranger*, the character Salamano lives alone with his unattractive dog, whom he appears to detest and whom he insults and mistreats, but whom he misses terribly when he dies. I suppose that Salamano's ill-treatment of the dog might be interpreted as a defence against an awareness of his dependence upon him.

If only the natural order could be reversed: first comes the loss, and then the love!

It is a curious fact that you can stop any stranger in the street with a dog and talk to him about his dog, when if you were to stop him without his dog and address him in the same fashion, he would probably express fear that you were a criminal lunatic and look around for the nearest policeman just in case. This is true not only in England but also (I have found) in France and America, or at least in New York. Not only are people willing to talk about their dogs but a positively eager and delighted to do so. Furthermore, what they have to say about their dogs is usually interesting, unlike what they have to say about their children.[2]

Once when we were walking Ramses to the Bois de Vincennes in Paris, when he was about five years old, a man in his thirties stopped to talk about his Yorkshire Terrier who had died the year before aged eight. With what tenderness he spoke of him, and with what continuing grief at his loss! It was as if he needed to speak, but only to people of whom he could be certain would not find his sorrow disproportionate or ridiculous. We fit the bill perfectly. Not only were we members of the dog-loving fraternity who have an instinctive sympathy for one another, but we had the very same breed of dog as his. I had a strange and irrational reaction to our encounter. Though, as I have said, I was only too aware of Ramses' mortality, I felt a peculiar pride that he was still alive, as if this were the

---

2 Surveys suggest that about a quarter of people in Britain with both dogs and children say they prefer their dogs to their children. From what I see of the conduct of many British children in the street, I cannot say that I am surprised or shocked by this.

consequence of some special virtue in us, and that the man who lost his dog to illness must have made some mistake and was therefore in part to blame. In some irrational way, I felt that Ramses was the healthier for the encounter.

All men are mortal, Socrates is a man, therefore Socrates is mortal: we all know the syllogism and we all know that it applies to us, yet we are obliged to live as if it were not true. I used to observe this contradiction between the knowledge of the truth and the unlivability of it, as it were, from the bow window of my study which overlooked the church, with Ramses sitting at my feet. The church was not used very much, except for some weddings and rather more frequently for funerals.

These funerals were very bourgeois, in a provincial way. A splendid hearse would draw up, preceded by a solemn professional mourner[3] dressed in a black swallow-tail coat, striped trousers, top hat and gloves. Following the hearse were several black mourning limousines, with the family of the deceased. Everyone would disappear into the church for a time, about half an hour on average, and then re-emerge, shaking the vicar's hand as they did so. They would then hang around at a loose end for a few minutes, waiting for the widow to depart to wherever the funeral collation was being held, chatting until then. The more important of them—that is to say the men of affairs, not necessarily the closest relatives of the deceased—would stand apart and consult their mobile telephones to find what messages they had missed during the ceremony. They gave the impression that the whole business had been an unnecessary and unwanted interruption of the day's schedule, and that the deceased should, like Lady Macbeth, have

---

3   I am fascinated by the idea of mourning as a profession, and have long wanted to interview a professional mourner. But I have never dared to approach one to do so.

died hereafter, that really he or she had no call to die at all, least of all at such a time as this, let the dead bury their dead, I am really too busy for this kind of thing, death has nothing to do with me or me with death, time to get back to work and draw a close to this foolish interruption.

This all seemed a very perfunctory end to a man's life, a life as important to him as mine is to me, having been (I do not doubt) as full of interest and passion as has mine. And yet, his funeral was clearly part of that very brief interregnum between being alive and being forgotten. The funeral was a stark reminder of our own unimportance; even Miss Havisham's mourning had to come to an end, if only with her own death. I picked up Ramses and cuddled him, though I could not explain why I did so at that particular moment. He was not displeased, though perhaps a little puzzled. He was, after all, a creature capable of absorbing any amount of love.

After Ramses' death, my wife and I were walking one day down the rue des Pyrénées in Paris when we passed an old lady out walking her dog, an apricot poodle who was fully grown but still evidently young, with that liquid movement of young dogs so beautiful to observe but which (alas) does not last long. We complimented the old lady on the charm of her dog, which she received with more pleasure than if we had complimented her herself, for at least our compliment was assuredly sincere. We started talking dog-talk.

She was well on in her eighties and the dog would live until she was a hundred; but she felt fully justified in having taken him as a puppy, not only because he alleviated (perhaps more than completely) her loneliness as a widow and gave her something—I hesitate to use the word someone—to live for, but because she had made suitable ar-

rangements for his care in the event of her death. She had
a younger friend whom the dog already liked, and would
give him a good and loving home.   *who*

The idea of this sensible arrangement did not altogether please me—not because there was anything wrong with
it, but because it made me reconsider our own relationship
with Ramses. If we believe that a dog can so easily transfer
its affections to another person and be perfectly happy after having done so, how genuine or deep can its love have
been for us? Is a dog's love what is called *cupboard love*,
that is to say signs of affection in return for food? I tried
to put this discomfiting question out of my mind. Much
of Ramses' affectionate behaviour was unrewarded except
by our own affection; and, after all, he came to us when
he was two, and for the subsequent thirteen years we did
not doubt his love for us, though he had previously loved
another family just as much, and in the same way, as he
loved us. We do not conclude from the fact that a widow
or widower remarries that she or he did not really love the
first spouse.

Nevertheless, these rational considerations left me
with a slight feeling that I was whistling in the wind, that
I was trying to reassure myself. There is no love without
uncertainty or willing self-deception:

> When my love swears that she is made of truth
> I do believe her though I know she lies,
> That she may think me some untutored youth,
> Unlearnèd in the world's false subtleties.

When Ramses died, we did not get another dog, as
friends had recommended beforehand that we should.
There were strictly practical reasons that we did not, but
these were not the main reason, which I knew not to be ra-

tional. We felt that to take another dog would be to betray his memory as a unique and irreplaceable being, though of course he was beyond the reach of such betrayal. We felt it would almost have been an acknowledgment that our attachment to him was excessive, absurd, a sign of a deficiency in our emotional lives.

I have told the story elsewhere (so I shall not repeat it) of the *chien professeur*, the Jack Russell Terrier of a teacher of badly-behaved or disturbed children whom we met in Paris out for a walk. His dog had a better effect in his classroom than the implementation of all the pedagogic techniques that he had learned put together, resulting in an immediate improvement in the behaviour of the unruly children. My experience in the prison in which I worked for fifteen years was not exactly analogous, but was nonetheless related. I found that to talk about a prisoner's dog, and to talk of my own, created an immediate rapport with the prisoner that could not be created in any other way, for example, by talking of his children. On the contrary, talk of that subject was inclined to induce a sense of anxiety, if not anger and guilt (directed at the mother or mothers of his child or children). I never heard a prisoner ask me to check on his behalf the safety of a child, but I was asked by several to do so on behalf of a dog. Likewise, no prisoner showed me a picture of his child, but several did so of their dogs.

Ramses was a very approachable dog, if I may so put it. Indeed, there was something about him, some canine charisma, that drew people to him. Of course, some people might say that this was a figment of our imagination, that we had become foolish fond old people, and that every person with a dog (I avoid the expression dog-owner) would say the same of his companion. But I do not think that they would necessarily be right: not all dogs are equally attractive to all people. Not every dog draws my attention in the street, for example; they must not only be physically attractive, but must manifest a personality to do so, and indeed the latter is more important than mere physical appearance. Red setters, for example, are very handsome dogs, indeed beautiful, but they seldom exhibit much individual personality. Indeed, it is the larger breeds that tend to have less charisma. Smaller dogs, though not the very smallest, have much more personality. The Jack Russell may not be the handsomest of dogs, but you never meet one that is as inert as, say, a Newfoundland. Oddly enough, there seems to be a vogue at the moment—both in Britain and France—of breeds that strike me as ugly, and who have not much personality to boot, French Bull-dogs, for example. There is a vogue also for vicious breeds, or those that can easily be trained to be such, whose own-ers or masters often come to resemble them: not Life imi-tating Art, but Man imitating Dog. This is consonant with the wave of self-mutilation that has overtaken the Western world in the name of self-expression, that is to say, pierc-ing, tattooing and the deliberate donning of ugly clothes. To paraphrase Milton:

> So farewell Hope, and with Hope, farewell Fear,
> Farewell remorse: all Good to me is lost;
> Ugliness be thou my Beauty.

Deliberately to adopt ugliness as an aesthetic abolishes, of course, the hope of achieving beauty, but also the fear of not being beautiful, with the great advantage that an aspi-ration to ugliness is very easily fulfilled.

Ramses drew people in the street to him. They petted

and whispered sweet nothings to him, and children adored him. What the charisma consisted of I can't quite say; it is in the nature of charisma that it should not be analysable. Certainly, Ramses exuded a curiosity about the world, an evident joy in being in it, and an assumption that love and attention were not so much his due (for he was a proud rather than an arrogant dog), as perfectly normal and as a matter of mere fact. Our basic stance towards the world affects the way the world treats us almost as much as the way the world treats us affects our basic stance towards it.

One incident, trivial in itself, remains strangely engraved on my mind and curiously evocative of emotion. It occurred when we were in North Wales with Ramses. We had rented a cottage in the village of Tal-y-bont a few miles from Bangor, with a wonderful view of the hills that at the time were dusted with snow like fine icing sugar. The cottage suited us perfectly: I could write and take Ramses for regular walks while my wife was away at work in the nearby hospital.

Strictly speaking, Ramses wasn't supposed to be there at all. When we answered the advertisement for the cottage, it said at the bottom, NO PETS. We are normally compliant with conditions laid down when the person laying them down has the perfect right to do so, and I experienced a slight pang of conscience when we lied about Ramses in order to be accepted as tenants. But guilt always calls forth rationalisation—even in the most unimaginative of persons. Thus, we decided that to call Ramses a pet was a gross understatement of his importance in our lives; besides which he was very clean and no trouble at all, so that it was simply irrational to exclude him. We therefore arrived at the cottage in two stages, my wife first to meet the landlady and have the keys presented to her, I arriving a little later with Ramses after my wife had given the all-clear. In the course of the following three months, the landlady called a couple of times to check that everything was all right (that we were not destroying her property), but she had always to give us advance notice of her visits, so that we had time to hide the evidence of Ramses' existence. Whether the landlady was fooled, I do not know; but since we were very good tenants, looking after her property with more care than we looked after our own, she did not rescind our tenancy.

The cottage was in Lon Ddwr, which I think means Water Lane. Certainly there was a nearby stone bridge over a stream. One day I was taking Ramses for his afternoon walk when I passed a young boy, just home from school and sill in his uniform, sitting on the low garden wall of his house.

'What's your dog's name?' he asked without any shyness.

He was a nice little boy, with a face that expressed immediate affection for Ramses. I told him that it was Ramses, and he gave a little laugh that was like the happy sound of a rill, and then he turned to go indoors to his mother.

Why has this tiny incident, so insignificant in itself, left a strong trace in my mind, when I have forgotten whole swathes of my life? Is forgetting—a very necessary function of the mind—a matter of chance, or is there some direction or purpose behind it (other than a general one), such as Freud suggested? No doubt both chance and direction are involved; it is not either-or.

Whatever the answer, the fact remains that I recall the incident perfectly and I still derive pleasure from doing so. I cannot say why this should be. Was it the innocent frankness of the boy, who was nevertheless already sophisticated enough to know to address me in English rather than in Welsh? His obvious goodwill towards an animal pleased me. But yet again, the pleasure of recollection is tinged with melancholy, as I recollect that the little boy who is forever sitting on his garden wall and forever asking me the question 'What's your dog's name', is by now a young adult, probably with a university degree and either pursuing further studies or working in goodness knows what capacity. When we come across innocence, we want to preserve it, which is possible only in our minds, not in external reality.

Memory preserves as amber preserves ancient insects. It is the finitude of the human mind compared with the infinitude of the world that leads us to have so many static memories. When I learned from a newspaper that the distinguished actor, Marius Goring, had died, I was shocked. He had remained in my memory as Angelo in *Measure for Measure*, in which part I had seen him in Stratford thirty-five years earlier, a middle-aged man in a short burgundy velvet tunic. It was as if my having seen him then (and never since) had acted as a preservative, and it had never occurred to me in the meantime that he must have aged.

Ramses had a talent to engender love at first sight. He did so in the case of Peter Bauer, the distinguished development economist, who was a tutor to the Nobel Prize-winner, Amartya Sen. He, Bauer, used to say that Mrs Thatcher's only two achievements were the destruction of the unions in Britain and her elevation of him to the House of Lords. He was so captivated by Ramses when he first met him that (according to others) he could not stop talking about him; a bachelor of eighty, though still attracted and attractive to women, he was like a child who, seeing a pretty baa-lamb in a field, badgers his mother to have one at home, the mother-figure in this case being his housekeeper. She refused to countenance a dog, for she said that it was she who would have to walk him and otherwise tend to him, while he – Lord Bauer – would have all the enjoyment of him, much as grandparents have the enjoyment of children without the responsibilities for them. But she said he could have a cat instead, as being more independent and less trouble than a dog, and she obtained one for him.

It was not the same thing at all. Even for a cat, the cat his housekeeper found was haughty, disdainful, stand-offish and superior, without, however, being independent. It displayed neither gratitude nor affection, like some children whom (alas) I could name. Sharper than a serpent's tooth was it to have an ungrateful cat—because it had claws to scratch antique furniture and upholstery. Peter came not merely to feel no affection for it, but actual aversion to it. His feelings never grew to the proportions of the narrator of Edgar Allan Poe's story, 'The Black Cat', but relations between them never progressed beyond wary indifference. It was like an indissoluble marriage of two people who live together but exchange no words. Because of our modern feelings about animals—so different from those about marriage—the cat could not simply be abandoned or put out to fend for itself. In short, Peter was stuck with it.

Humanity can be divided into four (it can also be divided into seven billion, that is to say as many people as there are in the world, since each of us is unique): those who love dogs, those who love cats, those who love both, and those who love neither. Dog-lovers and cat-lovers in their archetypal forms are looking for different qualities in what the French call, with accurate concision, their *animaux de compagnie*. The relations between cats and dogs mirror those of their *êtres humains de compagnie*. There are dogs that can't stand cats, and cats that can't stand dogs, there are dogs and cats (a small minority, it is true) that are friends, and there are dogs and cats that tolerate, but are indifferent to, one another. Pure dog-lovers and pure cat-lovers can never agree about each other's predilections. Dog-lovers see no point in cats, but it is precisely what dog-lovers love in dogs that cat-lovers reprehend. Dogs are demanding; dogs are dependent. You cannot leave a dog for a weekend as you can a cat. You have either to take it with you or make alternative arrangements (not always easy to do), or not go at all. Thus, a dog limits you in a way that a cat does not. In the cat-lover's eyes, a dog's dependence is a character-fault, nothing but a nuisance, a sign of irredeemable inferiority as a species, its apparent love mere fawning, hypocritical, Uriah Heep-like. It does not choose to be affectionate, it has to be affectionate if it is to survive; therefore, its apparent affection, being purely instrumental, is worthless or worse than worthless. Whereas a cat, etc., etc.

A cat is a torturer of mice, a denuder of birds in the garden. It is true that Christopher Smart saw in the cat's playing with mice evidence of its attachment to fair play, giving mice a sporting chance to escape rather than face certain death, thereby not quite extinguishing hope, but this is ridiculous, mere special-pleading. A well-fed cat does not need mice for food; if it had any finer feelings, it would leave the mice alone in the first place. What harm have mice ever done to cats, that they should persecute them so? As for birds, the case against cats is even more damning, insofar as we value birds more than mice. It has been established that the decline in the number of garden birds is in no small part due to the excessive number of cats. It is true that dogs sometimes chase birds, but this is clearly just for fun because they rarely catch them, and they know this from experience. Gun dogs are at worst accessories after the fact: they are not wanton bird-killers like cats. And if it is lack of affection or emotional distance that you want in an animal, why not go the whole hog, to mix a metaphor, and take a reptile—as increasingly many people do?

The argument between dog- and cat-lovers is without end, which is not to say that it is without point. Suffice it to say that I prefer dogs.

Ramses' experience of human beings was uniformly good. To adapt slightly Falstaff's view of himself, that he was not only witty in himself but the cause of wit in others, Ramses was not only good in himself, but a cause of goodness in others. But though he never experienced any cruelty or humans other than of a decent nature, it was clear that he did not like all people equally and preferred some to others. He had a very acute sense of who really liked dogs and who did not, as most dogs do, even when they have suffered nothing at human hands. He was particularly fond of our cleaning lady, for example, who came three times a week and lessened his loneliness. He greeted her with unmistakable signs of ecstasy, more enthusiastically than he greeted any other regular visitor to our house. Of course, the affection was reciprocated, otherwise Ramses would hardly have reacted in this way. Indeed, so great was the love between them that we had no hesitation in leaving Ramses to her care, when we were obliged to leave him behind when we went away. With her, we knew that he would not unduly miss us; and when we returned and fetched him from her house, we usually found him sitting comfortably on a sofa between her and her husband, watching television—which he never had the opportunity to do in our house.

The only people who seemed to dislike Ramses as a matter of course, though without doing him any harm, were young Moslems of Pakistani descent whom we encountered in numbers in a public park about three miles from our house. If he approached them at the end of his extendable lead, they shied away, not so much in fear as in disgust. The Islamic attitude toward dogs, at least in the mainstream (but much less so in the upper classes, besides which there must be variations in a population so large) is not very favourable. According to *The Religion of Islam: A Comprehensive Discussion of the Sources, Principles and Practice of Islam*, by Maulana Muhammad Ali, a firm believer but not an obvious fanatic, published in Lahore in 1952, Moslems are allowed to keep dogs, but only if they perform some useful function such as guarding a house, herding sheep, and so forth. They may not be kept in the house purely for pleasure or companionship. It is certainly not difficult to find anti-dog pronouncements by Moslem clerics, and the question whether Moslems may keep dogs (as pets) is always discussed by them in what one might call a pre-Enlightenment way, that is to say that the answer to the question is to be found in pre-existing sources, not as a source of previous wisdom but as a source of authority, ultimately descending from Mohammed himself. Never is there any independent thought, except by scholastic re-interpretation of previous opinions and commentary. The question thus boils down to this: whether the Koran, the Sunna or the Hadith permit you to keep a dog as a pet. If the answer is yes, you can; if no, you can't. (Rabbinic Judaism, by the way, is similar, though with different authorities.) The Enlightenment has been much criticised, no doubt often with justice, for it was often philosophically and psychologically shallow, but if anyone were to doubt the need for some kind of Enlightenment, he would do well to read Moslem clerics' discussions of the dog question to be found on the internet. And whatever the 'correct' doctrine of dogs in Islam may be, an unfavourable attitude had certainly communicated itself to the young Moslems in the park that I encountered.[4]

There are also 'enlightened' objections to the keeping of dogs. Since dogs require feeding, emit greenhouse gases, and are not strictly necessary in the crudely utilitarian sense, it is environmentally irresponsible (so some would argue) to keep a dog. But while everyone is, or should be, against the wilful destruction of the environment, there is a kind of pagan, proto-totalitarian puritanism about extreme environmentalism, which so venerates the earth, or at least the surface of the earth, that any human activity that could conceivably cause harm to it is the equivalent of haram, forbidden, in Islam. The desire to forbid the pleasure of others is a recurrent, if not quite constant, temptation of thinking mankind (I know, because I sometimes succumb to the temptation myself), and of course desires are always on the lookout for justifications—or rationalisations. The preservation of the environment is a perfect justification in this respect, for it is compatible with almost anything, including the placement of hideous, noisy bird-mincing wind turbines in beauty spots, which have the inestimable side-advantage of making it less worthwhile to go to see them. The Duke of Wellington said about the coming of the railways that they, railways, were reprehensible, because they would encourage the lower orders to move

---

4 In their books about the deaths of their dogs, Jean Grenier (*Sur la mort d'un chien*, 1957) and Jules Roy (*La Mort de Mao*, 1969), who were both friends of Albert Camus, allude to the Moslem dislike of dogs. Both authors lived long in Algeria. (Roy was born and brought up there.) I have been both alarmed and pleased by the many similarities of what they and I have to say, alarmed because I am far from being original, but pleased because I am far from being unusual. I take refuge in Doctor Johnson's dictum that we have more often to be reminded than informed.

about unnecessarily. In the name of the future, we are not to enjoy the present. But, as Feste says in *Twelfth Night*:

Present mirth hath present laughter,
What's to come is still unsure...

Prudence and providence are virtues, no doubt, but the uncertainty of the future easily makes what appears to have been prudent or provident turn out in practice to have been their opposite. In short, I prefer dogs to be out of the manger than in it.

All the same, I did have qualms, as I have indicated, or what Catholics call doubts, about the intensity of our feelings for, and relationship with, Ramses. Was it the sign of something deficient in, or missing from, our lives? My epigraph from Edgar Allan Poe suggests that this intensity was by no means unprecedented, but Edgar Allan Poe was hardly a model of psychological balance or stability.

In my own case, I can easily, and at least plausibly, trace my own love of dogs and ease of relationship with them to my childhood. I grew up in a loveless household. My parents never spoke to one another, not a single word do I remember having passed between them even when we went on holiday together. I love silence, but not the kind of silence that has a positive, hostile quality. Nor do I remember any single instance of affection expressed towards me, either physically or verbally. As children suppose that the conditions in which they are raised are perfectly normal, I found it astonishing, almost disturbing, when in other households I heard people speak to one another.

Had it not been for our dog, Chips, I should not have known love, either given or received. On to him I could pour all the affection of my nature. I loved him passionately, and was never happier than when taking him for a walk. (In those days it was still safe for a boy of nine to go out on his own.) Chips never rejected me, was never disapproving or angry, never made me feel I was a burden; on the contrary, I could confide in him, certain that he would understand.

Although we cannot make our childhoods an alibi for a failed life, except in the most extreme conditions (which were not mine), men are to a degree masters of their own fate; yet, it would be vain to deny that our childhoods have a lingering effect on our lives. In my case, this effect was an ease with dogs and an awkwardness with people. From my mother's refusal to touch me, except in medical circumstances, when some kind of bandage or such like was required, or express any kind of love in my formative years, I have ever since derived an embarrassment about, even a horror of, physical contact and emotional display by, with or towards others, difficult (though not quite impossible, thanks to the human faculty of consciousness) to overcome: whereas with dogs, I find it difficult to resist the impulse to embrace them, at least in that they are minimally attractive, as most of them are.

I shall return in a little while to this emotional deformation which is by no means uncommon.

It is with a certain embarrassment, but in the interest of truth, that I now turn to the names of endearment that we gave to Ramses. No doubt psychologists and anthropologists have written many profound, learned, boring and incomprehensible books about the human propensity to give nicknames both to those whom they love and those whom they hate. Euphemism, taboo and magical thinking are cognate but not identical phenomena, all being means by which we try to change the nature of reality by means of words and silences. (One could write a social history of any country by reference to the reigning euphemisms of successive ages. The use of sex-work instead for prostitution, and job-seekers for the unemployed, will tell future social historians something about our mentality.) In the case of Ramses, our other names for him were a mark of our deep affection for him.

I was walking behind Ramses one day when it occurred to me that he had something in common with, or reminiscent of, Piglet, that is to say the Piglet of Ernest Shepard's illustrations of *Winnie-the-Pooh*. These illustrations are what Shepard is mainly remembered for, and like Conan Doyle who is remembered above all for Sherlock Holmes, he came to detest the work that gave him his modest immortality. As a child, I tried to learn to draw by copying Shepard's illustrations (and Sir John Tenniel's of Alice), but I never got very far, and I have since regressed even from the slight progress that I made.

Shepard's disdain for his own work notwithstanding, I find it depressing that his Pooh illustrations have been replaced almost entirely by Disney's crude adaptations of them. Shepard's originals are tender and monochrome, where Disney's adaptations of them are crude and garish. If I say this to parents, they reply that their children are immediately drawn to the brightly coloured Disney versions, an argument that illustrates how we have sentimentalised children by making them authorities. It is precisely because they are naturally drawn to the crude and bright that they should be given something more subtle, for the aesthetic sense needs its education too, if people are not to remain in their aesthetic infancy. It is the same with food: if you give children only what they ask for, which of course avoids a lot of short-term irritation or conflict, they will never grow out of their childish tastes, which will make them fat and unhealthy and deny them the far greater and more varied pleasures of the table.

Ramses must have reminded me of Shepard's Piglet very soon after he came to us, for I do not remember a time when we did not call him Piglet as well as Ramses. And from Piglet, we derived many other names and diminutives for him. He soon became Piggy and then Piggy-Wig or Piggy-Wiggy. When we spoke of him between ourselves, we referred to him as The Pig or The Piglet. (Piggy-Wig derived, of course, from Lear's *The Owl and the Pussy-Cat*: 'And there in a wood a piggy-wig stood...') And then he became, no name being used on all or even consecutive occasions, Piggy-paws and Paws, after which we sometimes referred to him as The Paws. For some reason, the word paws has happy and even tender connotations, unlike the word claws which has harsh and cruel ones. I never called Ramses Paws without remembering a character in George Bernard Shaw's early novel, *An Unsocial Socialist*, which I read under the influence of an admired English teacher at school, who later became a professor, and who thought that Shaw was the greatest dramatist in English since Shakespeare. (Only much later did I realise that this was not saying very much.) The character was called, or rather called himself, *Smilash*, a contraction and amalgamation of the words *smile* and *eyelash*, thinking that everyone would like him because of the pleasant connotations of these two words. In the case of Ramses, of course, the direction was from affection to nickname rather than the other way round. (Shaw was not a very good novelist, which is why he changed literary genre.)

In public, however, we always called him by his official name, the name that appeared on his passport and on his veterinary records, Ramses. It was more dignified—for us, not for him—because we did not want to reveal our soppiness in plain hearing.

Ramses was a healthy dog and so his veterinary records were not extensive. They related mainly to his im-
munisations and to the insertion of an electronic chip, a
requirement for travel abroad, as well as useful if he were
ever lost. He also had collars and harnesses, two of which
we kept as relics after his death. His medallion with his
name and address and our telephone numbers was buried
with him.

Not surprisingly, he was rather subdued in the vet's
waiting room. The other dogs were similarly subdued and
very well-behaved, and never barked, let alone snarled or
fought. It was as if they knew that something serious was
afoot, something not very pleasant, perhaps, but for their
own good, and therefore no occasion for silly quarrels.
Cats, by contrast, had to be kept in wire or plastic cages.
Unlike dogs, they could not be counted on to rise to the
occasion and behave themselves.

I was pleased to see that on Ramses' veterinary records,
we were inscribed as his Mum and Dad rather than as his
owners. I am sure that parenthood was not ascribed to us
uniquely. Then, as was my wont, I began to worry whether
a society in which people were so deeply attached to their
animals was one in which human relations were corre-
spondingly difficult—more difficult than they had always
been—even, or especially, with their children.

I thought of all my friends, many of whom had great
difficulties in their relations with their children, despite
having been good and conscientious parents. Few of them
had had relations that were straightforward or uncomplicated, though wherever they had, their children were the
greatest possible source of joy. But there were also cases,
perhaps more of them, of such inharmonious or conflict-

ual relations that their children were almost a prolonged torture to them, though (and it was this that made it so chronically yet exquisitely painful) still loved. In many cases, it seemed almost as if Man's primordial and permanent attachment to his children were Nature's revenge on his arrogance and hubris as a species, a nasty and protracted joke.

And here I am speaking of good parents, those who were loving, sensitive, sensible and responsible. In my work, I met many who were none of these things, who were cruel or careless or callous, who scarred their own children by their own selfishness or stupidity and made one wonder why they had children in the first place, so neglectful of or hostile to them were they.

Naturally, I wondered whether, had I been born at any other time or place, things would have been different, that relations between parents and children—on average, for there is no new thing under the sun—would have been more uncomplicated and affectionate; and if so, whether our generations are uniquely incompetent in the matter of child-rearing, despite, or even because of, our vaunted or supposed increase in psychological knowledge, or at least research. Could it be, indeed, that an instinctual knowledge of how to bring up children is like the blush of a grape, ruined by the touch of self-conscious interrogation? Of course, if the premise is wrong—that relations between parents and children are more difficult than they once were—then it is useless to speculate along these lines. There is plenty of literary evidence—Dickens, Turgenev, Gosse come straight to mind—or to my mind at any rate— that this might not be so, and even that the opposite might be the case.

Nevertheless, I could not help but observe that the atmosphere in a vet's waiting room is consistently and considerably more pleasant than that in a doctor's waiting room, at least in England.

Why should this be?

In the first place, in the vet's waiting room, there is a fellowship of unclouded love which is certainly not the case in a doctor's waiting room. Everyone is at the vet because of his or her unselfish love of a cherished creature; and because of this love, each has empathy for all, and all have empathy for each. If a dog begins to misbehave slightly, which is seldom, everyone present makes allowances for it and feels for its owner.

No such allowances are made for those who behave badly in the doctor's waiting room, for example, a fractious child in the charge of a weak or feckless mother, an unwashed man smelling of alcohol, or a demanding drug addict who resorts to threats if he doesn't get his way. The atmosphere is in any case much less benign, much tenser than in a vet's waiting room, as if in the former, people are expecting to be misdiagnosed or in some way maltreated. Part of the reason for the difference, no doubt, is that people have to pay at the vet's and expect to do so, whereas, at the doctor's they are paupers, in control of nothing, and often treated more as a nuisance, or as malingerers trying to cheat their way to a privilege, than as equals or responsible adults. There is, it is true, a charity, the People's Dispensary for Sick Animals, for the treatment of the pets of those who cannot or will not pay for it themselves; but overall, the PDSA plays a small part in the veterinary care of the nation's domestic animals. By contrast, the role of the People's Dispensary for Sick Humans is overwhelming in the medical care of human beings.

Ramses shivered, or trembled, as we waited, although he had had no very bad experience of vets. It was as if he knew that one day something bad would happen to him there and in his prevision he was quite right.

One day we were waiting our turn at the vet's, when a little girl entered with her father, carrying a small cage in which there was a hamster. It was obvious to all present that the hamster was very sick, nigh unto death, and that for it, as Mistress Quickly put it with regard to Falstaff, there was only one way. The little creature was very inert—not that hamsters seem to me to be very active at the best of times.

Father, daughter and hamster were called straight into the vet's consulting room, seemingly out of turn, as an emergency as it were: not that any of us minded, for we wanted the inevitable denouement to occur as soon as possible for the little girl's sake. Everyone in the waiting room looked down at his feet, and there was complete silence in the waiting room as the consultation took place.

The silence did not last long. The little girl emerged sobbing with an empty cage, her father's consoling arm around her. Our interest in our shoes intensified as they left, which of course was straightaway after the father had paid. The sombre atmosphere lingered for a while, as if we were all contemplating our own mortality.

The little girl's love for her hamster was unmistakably real and deep. By now she must be a grown woman, perhaps with children of her own. Does she remember her hamster or her grief for it? Is the experience of such a loss educative and formative of character? It is sometimes said that a loss of the sense of the tragic is at the root of the deformations of modernity, as is the shallow belief that life can and is expected to be lived with the ease of a hot knife slicing through butter: in which case, one might expect a little girl who had, at an early age, loved and lost, would have as an adult a better and deeper character than one who hadn't. Whether or not this is so, I cannot say. I have been so affected—or is it infected?—by the methodology of modern medicine that I find it difficult to accept any generalisation (unless I make it myself in the heat of a discussion) that is not backed up by proper evidence. As soon as I raise a question, such as the deepening effect on character of the experience of loss in childhood, I immediately demand a scientific trial, with proper controls, to prove that it does (or doesn't). My feeling or suspicion, however strong, that it does is not sufficient, as once it might have seemed to me. Thus conscience—or what we now call consciousness—makes cowards of us all, and we become afraid of our own common sense judgments. But life cannot be conducted as a double-blind trial; we have to take a hundred leaps in the dark each day, and any father who denied his daughter the pleasures of having a hamster on the grounds that no proper scientific evidence existed to demonstrate the long-term benefits of hamster ownership, or for that matter its possible harms, would rightly be regarded as a monster of fatuous cerebration.

Perhaps I am such a monster, for the little girl's love of her hamster raised a question in my mind, of a type that I try to push away but that returns unbidden, namely that since I found it difficult to believe that a hamster had sufficient mental capacity to return her affection, but since she clearly believed that it did, was I under the same kind of illusion with Ramses, not suffering the illusion but rather enjoying it? I took the short Johnsonian way with metaphysical questions: I knew that Ramses loved me, and there's an end on it. But such summary dismissals do not entirely convince.

As I have mentioned, Ramses was generally a healthy dog, but he suffered one memorable, if very short, illness.

When my wife retired from her permanent post in her hospital, she threw a party for her erstwhile staff in our house. Much as I enjoy intimate dinner parties (so that I am neither entirely a recluse nor a misanthrope), I detest parties of—if I may so put it—the party type. They bore me terribly, far more than my own company, and I do not see the point of them. The noise is abominable, especially if there is music, and the conversation, if you can make it out, is banal. I particularly detest literary parties, because everyone's eyes are constantly swivelling to see whether there is someone more important or more useful to his career than you on the horizon, to whom he would therefore much rather be speaking. I have no sooner to enter a room in which a party is taking place than for my mind to empty completely of anything to say. I immediately become a bore, or more of a bore than usual. As for orgies, once you've seen one, you've seen them all.

My wife's party, therefore, was the first and only party that we had either held or would ever hold. As such parties go, it was a very good one. We had arranged for friends to come and mix and serve cocktails, which none of us was accustomed to drinking and whose potency came to us as a surprise. There is nothing like a cocktail to reduce shyness or other social inhibitions. In fact, it was the only good, which is to say enjoyable, party that I have ever attended.

But Ramses did not enjoy it. This was not only because it could not have been much fun being surrounded by many noisy giants (as humans must have appeared to him), but because he had ceased to be the centre of our affectionate attention, as by now he was of customary right. Halfway through the party, someone noticed that Ramses could not move his back legs, that they were paralysed, and called this to our notice. We were very worried, not to say panic-struck, all the more so because a vet had told us that Yorkshire Terriers were prone to such paralysis because of a genetic disorder of their lumbar vertebrae. We lifted our poor little dog up tenderly and put him gently in his basket. We tried to raise his spirits with bits of smoked salmon and sausages, but he showed no interest in them. We thought we would have to rush him to Bristol, where there was an MRI scanner for dogs (and no doubt for cats as well), whose heavy fees we were prepared to pay, and then to find a canine orthopaedic surgeon, or rather an orthopaedic surgeon for canines, one specialising in back surgery, to operate on him. But then an Irish child psychiatrist, a friend of my wife's, over from Ireland specially for the party, made a firm diagnosis: hysterical conversion disorder of the kind that Freud saw in *fin de siècle* Vienna (and which he signally failed to cure). We did not believe her: surely, no mere animal had a psyche as complex as those of the rich and bored ladies of Vienna?

But the child psychiatrist was quite right. As soon as the party was over and every guest except the child psychiatrist had gone home, Ramses hopped out of his basket as spry as ever, and I was even able to take him for his accustomed walk as if nothing had ever been wrong with him.

The diagnosis of hysterical conversion is nowadays a controversial one, and there has long been a campaign for the abandonment of the word hysteria and its cognates as being inherently derogatory rather than scientifically descriptive, derogatory especially of women who suffered more from it (at least until the First World War). But it is easier to change the words with which we describe phenomena than to change the phenomena themselves. It is true that the hysterical paralysis of limbs (in humans) is seen much less frequently than it once was, but that is not the issue. I saw such cases from time to time, in fact, not very long before Ramses' own episode of paralysis. It was in a lady of Pakistani Punjabi origin who developed an hysterical paralysis after her detested and tyrannical husband retired from work and had a heart attack, after which she was expected to wait hand and foot on him even more assiduously than before. Her only defence against such domestic slavery was to become incapacitated herself. She improved in hospital until she could walk normally but relapsed immediate on her discharge home. Although the conclusions to be drawn from this were perfectly obvious, neither she, nor her husband, nor her grown-up children, drew them. To have done so would have been to admit that her life had been hell for years, and this none of them wanted to do. A paralysed leg was the only solution.

Restored to his proper position in our household, Ramses never relapsed.

Ramses trusted us completely, which implied some kind of awareness of our wholly benevolent intentions towards him. Once, when he had something stuck in his throat, he permitted, without in the least flinching, my wife to retrieve it, as if he knew that she was helping him. When in France a tick attached itself to his cheek and grew fat with his blood (the existence of ticks ought to be enough to preserve anyone from Nature mysticism), he let us remove it, we having learnt from the internet how to do so. And though he was by no means a cowardly dog—I remember him at the age of thirteen or fourteen seeing off two very large dogs that had strayed on to our land in France, which he considered his own territory, the two large dogs fleeing his righteous anger in terror—he once jumped straight into my arms when, out for a walk, an unseen hound of gigantic size, a real Hound of the Basker-villes, to judge by the timbre of his voice, delivered himself of a single ferocious bark. Ramses knew that I would protect him, with my life if necessary.

My wife and I sometimes had an absurd discussion which I suspect many dog owners have: namely, if one of us and Ramses were in danger, which of us would the other rescue first? Behind the jocularity of the question, however, was an abiding fear that our love for him was absurd, disproportionate. Another question with which I used to torture myself when out walking him was whether I would sacrifice him to save the life of one, or two, or a million strangers? This was an absurd question, of course (perhaps philosophers would call it a thought experiment, in which an abstract moral principle is tested to its *reductio ad absurdum*), for no such situation could ever occur. But silly as the question was, it recurred to me over and over, and my answer revealed the difference between my head and heart. I knew that I should have to decide in favour of the humans, whether one or many, but I should do so against the inclination of my heart. This suggests that love is too particularised to be used as a guiding principle of political action, at least in my case and that of practically everyone I have ever met. No doubt there are a few people who are able to feel charitable towards huge abstract categories such as humanity, probably through natural inclination rather than as a result of ratiocination; but in general, whenever I hear someone claim to love humanity, my teeth are set on edge. Such people have often proved themselves to be capable of any cruelty, provided only that they can persuade themselves (as usually they can) that their cruelty is for the general good. Millions have been murdered for the general good.

I also used to think about the amount of money that we should be prepared to spend on treatment for Ramses should he fall ill of an expensively curable disease. We never, in fact, had to spend very much; but would it have been right to spend a great deal on a dog when that same amount might have saved a lot of human life? (I work on the supposition, not altogether well founded, that charitable donations are used for the ostensible ends of charities.)

I met a man one day out walking his dog, a Jack Russell, and we fell to talking—of dogs, of course. He was a long-distance lorry driver, well enough paid but not fabulously rich. When his dog had been a puppy, a vet discovered that he had a hole in his heart. Without a moment's hesitation, he had agreed to pay £3000 for the corrective surgery (heart surgery for dogs, I didn't even know that it existed!), and he did not regret it in the slightest, indeed it was the best use of money that he had ever found, although it meant that he could not go on holiday for a couple of years.

The puppy had obviously captured his heart very quickly. His owner said he could not have borne his death, particularly when he knew that he could be saved. If he had to spend the same money again, he would do so.

Who is there to say that he had spent his money frivolously or immorally and that he should have spent it in some other way? It is true that the love of dogs in general is usually more genuine than the love of humanity in general, but every person with a dog loves his or her dog in particular, and is prepared to go to much greater lengths to save it than for anybody else's dog. For those strange people who do not like dogs, or who even *dis*like them, it might seem preposterous, extravagant, sentimental for a man of modest means to spend so much money on a dog, but on what (in their opinion) *should* he have spent it? Why fix on him as an example of absurd expenditure? You have only to go into a crowded shopping street—I should perhaps have written, you *had* only to go into a crowded shopping street, for I write this in the midst of an epidemic that, at least temporarily, has made such streets a thing of the past—to see people searching for new possessions, new but very similar to ones of which they already have more than a sufficiency, as if they expected them to bring them contentment or happiness at last. The insolvent in pursuit of the unnecessary: to judge by their appearance, they are not even very discriminating in their purchases, and repeatedly fall for the illusion that just one more purchase will supply what the rest of their life has not.

Compare this with the man who has made a large financial sacrifice for his dog. He has done so in pursuit of one of the greatest ends of human life, perhaps the greatest end, namely love: and not only his only, but a love that he knows beyond reasonable doubt will be reciprocated. If ever there were a man who chose being before having, it was my interlocutor. He had used his scant resources to obtain something non-material, and far from being foolish, he was admirable.

Had he not told me about the operation, incidentally, I should not have guessed: his Jack Russell was as lively, inquisitive, active and alert as Jack Russells usually are.

I did not enquire whether he would have been outraged if he had had to pay five pounds to consult a doctor for himself. *Free at the point of use* has long been a kind of British religious mantra with regard to their own health care, but I did not explore this potential inconsistency—for none of us is wholly consistent in his thoughts or feelings, and I wanted to keep my admiration for the owner of the Jack Russell entire and intact.

Instead, after I left him, I constructed in my mind an ideological justification for a National Veterinary Service to match the National Health Service, a system to be paid for from general taxation (or rather, general borrowing) and available to everyone equally without further cost to himself, give or take a minor charge or two. After all, the NHS does not merely save lives in danger but acts to fulfil the desires of at least certain categories of people, for example those of people who want to change their sex.

There is little doubt that the companionship of a dog improves the quality of and extends the life of people, especially the elderly. A dog in a care home for the elderly improves the lives even of those with Alzheimer's disease. Dogs increase the time that people devote to exercise. Given, then, that the keeping of a dog, independent of all the other pleasures that it gives, can be regarded as medically beneficial, why should anyone—especially, of course, the poor—have to pay for a dog's veterinary treatment, when a dog's health is preservative of his own? Surely, the system of private veterinary care discriminates against the poor and discourages them from the keeping of a health-giving dog, or if they keep one, from preserving it in optimal health? I would imagine that somewhere there are statistics proving the dogs of the poor do not live as long as the dogs of the rich.

Enough said. I come now to the very painful subject, that of the death of Ramses. Although it was now so long ago, I still recall it with sorrow admixed with more than a little guilt.

I suppose, looking back on it, that his final illness started, or had its origin, while we were away in Mexico, having taken a few days rest after I gave a talk in Los Angeles. We had left Ramses in the care of another of his favourite people, someone on whom we could depend. While we were away, we received a message that he was not well: a severe attack of diarrhoea necessitating treatment by a vet. He was dehydrated, and it took some time to restore him to apparent good health.

When we returned, he seemed well and we thought no more of it; for though he was now old for a dog, and though at a merely intellectual level we knew that he could not live many years longer, we put the real possibility of his death from our minds. Had not the life expectancy of dogs, after all, increased *pari passu* with that of human beings? We preferred to believe in some kind of Zeno's paradox with regard to life expectancy. The latter, though it shortens with age, at least after infancy, never falls to zero, and therefore, like the arrow, never arrives at its destination, which is death. Thus, Ramses would never die and we should have him with us always.

But though seemingly restored to health, decline had set in. He was not so eager to go for a walk as he had been, and when he did go, he wanted to return home sooner. His appetite, having been consistent throughout his life (never excessive), was reduced. He slept more, though he remained as affectionate as ever when he woke. Where once he would have jumped onto our laps while we were sitting, he now had to be lifted. We ascribed this, of course, to the old bones from which we ourselves were beginning to suffer: an inconvenience, then, rather than a danger.

I cannot say when, exactly, we realised that he was ill rather than merely aging, or when a vet first told us the bad news. I think it was in France, at the vet in the small town, seven miles from our very isolated house.

We had been to that vet several times before. On one occasion, I remember, I discovered to my indignation that there was another Yorkshire Terrier registered with the practice of the name of Ramses. What shameless plagiarism or imitation! Couldn't people think up a dog's name for themselves? That the false or bogus Ramses was of the same breed as the true compounded the offence. I was obliged to calm my outrage by consoling myself that imitation was the sincerest form of flattery and that the False Ramses could not possibly be the equal of the True Ramses.

Two or three years after Ramses died, I had to return to that vet in strange circumstances. A Pyrenean mountain dog, a kind of cream-coloured Newfoundland, had wandered on to our land and appeared lost. He was very large and immediately began to follow me about. He was evidently well-looked after and not the kind of dog that anyone would wilfully abandon. He had no collar and, therefore, no medallion with his name and address. What to do? I fed him, and since it was already dusk I decided to wait until morning to see whether he had left. Unfortunately, he was still there in the morning.

I happened to be on my own in the house at the time, and telephoned my sister-in-law for advice. She very sensibly suggested that I take him to the vet, for it was likely that such a dog had been microchipped. I therefore put, or squeezed, him into the back of our small car, which he almost filled. He was reluctant to get in and I had to keep prodding him to do so while encouraging him with an unctuous voice. Luckily he was so passive, as very large long-haired dogs tend to be, that eventually I was able to coax him in.

How different from Ramses, who liked nothing better than a ride in the car! The words 'Are you coming, Piggy?' would cause him an immediate access of pleasurable excitement. He would jump up and down and rush into the car as soon as a door was opened. Generally, he sat on our lap on the passenger's side, but sometimes he would put his front paws on the window ledge and watch the world go by with his usual intensity of interest. He was actually quite a well-travelled dog, accompanying us to the Hebrides and through France, Switzerland, Germany, Belgium and Holland. He was also very well-behaved and we could take him anywhere, for example, to *La Coupole*, the celebrated Parisian restaurant, where he sat quietly and contentedly on the banquette.

Our house in France was nearly eight hundred miles from our house in England, and he sat on our lap the whole way, a great comfort and curiously enough reduced the tedium of the long drive—though it would be difficult to point to anything that he actually did to reduce it. When before her retirement my wife was on duty at night and was called at three or four in the morning to a police station ten or twenty miles away to assess the sanity or otherwise of someone who had been taken into custody having committed an act against the law—anything from smashing a window to stabbing someone to death—she would take Ramses with her for company and even, dangerously, let him sit on her lap as she drove.[5] His presence much reduced the unpleasantness of the hour for her, and we even joked that he came along to give a second opinion—as Dr. Ramses or Dr. Piglet. After all, he *was* a very good judge of character.

We also remarked on an unexpected faculty of his when we drove home from far away. He would sleep on our lap for much of the journey but wake suddenly when we were about a mile from home. It happened so many times that it could not just have been a coincidence. How did he know to wake? Was it some tensing or relaxation of our thigh muscles that he detected, some odour that we emitted, some change in the tone of our voices that he heard? He appeared fast asleep until then and was of course without visual clues. Perhaps the Society for Psy-

---

5 Jules Roy relates something similar – as far as driving is concerned – in his book, *La Mort de Mao.*

chical Research has already investigated the phenomenon.

Another of his occult faculties was the awareness of an approaching thunderstorm. Like most dogs, he hated thunderstorms. Ramses taught us what the expression *climbing the walls* meant: it meant climbing the walls, or at least trying to. Dogs are not climbing animals, but during a thunderstorm, Ramses would try to scramble up the nearest wall. He was extremely difficult, not to say impossible, to console during a thunderstorm. For once we could not hold him in our embrace, as he would try to wriggle free, though freeing himself did not calm him either.

When a thunderstorm happened at night, we would put Ramses under the bedclothes in the hope that the darkness and comparative silence would allay his fears. But they did not; whatever it was in the atmosphere that alarmed him, it penetrated into the bowels of the bed, where he kept up his frightened squirming. It was evidently not the thunderclaps or lightning alone that so disturbed him, for when they happened they did not seem to cause any exacerbation or heightening of his anxiety, which in any case began well before the storm declared itself to us—mere insensitive humans. In fact, he was like a barometer that shows a sudden drop in pressure premonitory to a storm. In other words, dogs have faculties to detect or sense things that humans do not have. It is well known that their sense of smell and hearing is more acute than ours, though their eyesight is much inferior; but by what sensory means do they detect the approach of a storm? Whatever they may be, they are more highly developed than in us, with our limited capacity (meteorologists excepted) to predict the approach of a storm.

During storms, we tried diazepam (Valium) to calm him and discovered that enormous doses, considering his size and weight, did not work. Doses that would have laid me low—I am exceptionally sensitive to such drugs—had no effect on him. Trying to calm him with drugs reminded me of a strange episode in my life.

I had been appointed for a few weeks as doctor to a community of expatriates in Nigeria. No sooner had I arrived than I faced the first test of my competence: the wife of a manager brought me a cat to put down. I had never put any creature down and had no idea how to do so. In a laboratory, I had 'sacrificed' guinea pigs (as the rather euphemistic expression in scientific writing has it), but by a method that I could hardly use in this case and which I shall not describe. However, I had read something in the newspapers of the fatal cocktail of drugs now used in American executions, the latter having been turned into quasi-medical procedures. I had in my little pharmacy a surprising quantity of barbiturates for injection and also of potassium chloride. I drew up quantities that I thought would surely put paid to the cat, even if given intraperitoneally rather than intravenously, without ever asking why the cat should be put down in the first place.

I injected the drugs and waited. Nothing happened. The wretched cat, held by its owner, continued to breathe normally. I assured the owner, without fully believing it myself, that the drugs took some time to act. This turned out not to be true; the cat shrugged them off. The owner looked at me appraisingly: what kind of doctor could I be if I couldn't even kill a cat properly? Despite the air-conditioning, which rendered the room as cool as a Scandinavian autumn, beads of perspiration formed on my forehead. Why couldn't the woman have drowned the cat in the nearby river, instead of bringing it to me to do her dirty work for her? Another injection, even larger, and then a third, was indicated. This brought about what nurses, after a patient's enema, used to call 'a good result'.

'Thank you, doctor,' said the woman, no doubt as traumatised as I. But her gratitude did not extend as far as disposal of the *corpus delicti*, which was left to me.

But to return to the lost Pyrenean mountain dog. Unlike Ramses, he was not a good traveller. Unfortunately, the track down to our house, which is in a valley, and the road to the town, are extremely winding. The dog was immediately car sick, not figuratively but literally, and brought up the pâté that, *faute de mieux*, I had fed him the evening before. The smell was horrible and when I recall it, I can still conjure it up in my mind's nose.

I nevertheless continued uninterruptedly to the vet. It turned out that the dog was indeed microchipped, and the vet called the owners who seemed remarkably casual about their dog's absence. They lived at some considerable distance (we have no close neighbours), and the dog, who seemed somewhat lumbering to me, had wandered far. But they came to collect him, bringing with them a pot of home-made apricot jam as a token of gratitude. This seemed a paltry reward for a smell in our car that was to endure for more than five years, cleaning with scented products making it only worse, sweet and vile. Despite my experience, however, my affection for dogs is undiminished.

By means of digression, I have put off for a short while my painful subject, the death of Ramses. It was in our house in France that he underwent a sudden deterioration. Previously, his decline had been gradual and consistent with aging, or so we thought. Taking him for a long walk in the forest surrounding our house, he would become tired and want to walk no further. I would pick him up, tuck him under my arm, and carry him home. He seemed quite content like this, and I felt that our physical closeness was more than merely physical. His trust in me was complete, though I carried him at what for me, *pro rata*, would have been a height of thirty or forty feet.

From time to time he had a cough, which we tried to ignore as one of those things, and his energy and appetite declined; and, as photographs now reveal to us with startling clarity, he lost weight. Almost certainly, we were in a state of denial, the ability to put out of mind an unpleasant reality that at some level or other is apprehended only too clearly. Thirty years earlier, I had disregarded my own illness in this fashion, when I too suffered a decline in my health similar to that of Ramses. As a young doctor, I believed it was others, not myself, who were subject to illness: for me to be ill was to reverse the natural order of things, besides which I had neither the time nor the inclination to be ill. What is more, I was surrounded at the time by people whose very specialty was the kind of illness from which I was suffering but who did not recognise it at the time until—quite by chance—I had a blood test that proved it, whereupon all those who had missed it before said that I was a textbook case (and indeed, a photograph of me at the time could be used in textbooks). The reason that they did not diagnose it was that our relations were not those of doctor to patient, and the way we look at things, at least within certain limits, depends on the context in which we look at them. And the context in which we looked at Ramses was one of wanting him to live as long as we, and therefore, he could not be seriously ill. The wish is father to the lack of thought.

Ramses would have little spasms of coughing. What did we think they were caused by? We put the question out of our minds as being too unpleasant to be decently asked. I should add that both my wife and I, thanks to our professional activities, had had more than an average experience of the facts of mortality. But as La Rochefoucauld said, we can stare neither at the sun nor at death for very long.

Self-deception, a very slippery concept philosophically, though we all recognise it when we see it (in others), is powerful but not all-powerful. I was away in Paris when my wife finally took Ramses to the vet, because it was no longer possible to deny that he was seriously ill. He was too exhausted now to walk more than a few yards and hardly ate or drank. Ramses, fifteen years old, was in heart and kidney failure.

He was admitted as an in-patient to the veterinary clinic and restored to balance by an intravenous drip and drugs. He had to stay two nights, and my wife describes a scene that, though I was not present to witness it, haunts me and fills my own heart with pain. Ramses spent one full day in the clinic and she went to visit him there. Not surprisingly, he was a picture of misery when she arrived, transformed into joy the moment he saw her. When it was time for her to go, however, she had to leave him behind. As she left, Ramses scrambled at the side of the cage, beseeching her to take him with her. His desperation was obvious, but she could do nothing. Not being Pharaoh, she could not harden her heart, but she had to do her duty and leave him in the clinic. It was for his good that she caused suffering both to him and herself in this way, but however much Man and dog may communicate by gesture, intuition and intonation, it requires words in propositional form to convey a painful necessity such as this parting. The scene as I describe it could not be more vivid in my mind than if I had been present and has almost the quality of a memory. If I rehearsed the scene often enough in my mind, I could probably persuade myself that I *had* actually been present, a warning against testimony in court taken many years after the events testified to.

There is, as it happens, a scene in literature that is not entirely dissimilar. It is in a short story, or novella, by Turgenev called *Mumu*. I have recommended this story to several people who did not know it and who said that they found the denouement almost too painful to read. If you want to know the power of the imagination to sympathise with the suffering of another, there is no better way than to read this story.

It is the story of Gerasim, the deaf-and-dumb serf of a capricious, egotistical, spoilt and tyrannical mistress. (Modelled on Turgenev's mother, Turgenev having early on in his life realised that a bad example was also, taken the right way, a good example, that is to say of what not to be and how not to behave.) The title of the story, Mumu, is the sound that Gerasim makes when he tries to speak and give a name to his dog. The very accuracy of this is testimony to Turgenev's compassion for someone whom many would overlook, not because they were themselves cruel or deliberately inconsiderate, but because they were impatient and unimaginative.

Gerasim's relations with the other serfs are not hostile, but he cannot, because of his impediment, draw close to them. The young woman, Tatiana, whom he tries to woo, is married off to another serf, a drunkard, on the orders of the mistress. Gerasim then rescues a dog, Mumu, to whom he becomes passionately attached, and who in turn loves him. Mumu is the object of all the love of his affectionate soul.

Gerasim, who once worked in the fields, is now a household serf and therefore lives in close proximity to his mistress's house. She is a bitter hypochondriac, whose concern for her own health is a distraction from the emptiness of her own life (as hypochondriasis often is). When she tries to pet Mumu, the dog snarls at her. Then one day, she wakes with a headache and blames Mumu's barking. She demands that the dog be sent away. But Gerasim keeps the dog in his room, from which, however, her whining when he is absent may still be heard. Hearing it, the mistress repeats her order that the dog be sent away. Gerasim now has no choice. He gives Mumu a last meal and then takes Mumu out on a boat on to the river. Mumu has no inkling of what is to happen to her, and still expresses her love for Gerasim. With breaking heart, he takes Mumu and drowns her. Gerasim, grieving beyond powers of expression, returns to his village of origin and the bitter, tyrannical old woman dies.

Great artist as he was, Turgenev does not tell us what to think or feel. The story itself is so powerful that any authorial commentary would be superfluous. A Russian friend of mine tells me that in Soviet times the story was printed by the millions to remind the population of the cruelties of Tsardom, a use to describe which the word *hypocritical* would be a gross understatement. But, as Stalin said, a single death is a tragedy, a million deaths is a statistic: and therefore, psychologically-speaking, the story of Gerasim more than cancelled out the whole of the Gulag. Thomas Carlyle was more honest. He said that *Mumu* was the greatest denunciation of arbitrary power ever written, which gives the story its permanent value, since—alas— arbitrary power is protean in its manifestations, from the highest level of the state to the lowest level of family life. The urge to tyrannise will never be expunged from all human hearts.

Turgenev did not choose the destruction of the relationship of Gerasim and Mumu at random, but because it was an example of the most harmless and unclouded love possible, that between man and dog. My wife and I were to live our own version of the story, Mumu.

I returned home from Paris on the day Ramses was released from the veterinary clinic. His misery was quite forgotten, and he was once again a happy dog. His health had greatly improved, and for a time he ran around as if fully-restored. Wherever he was for more than a few days, Ramses established a routine for himself and now he went on his usual tour of inspection of the property, taking his accustomed route. He trotted up the track from the main house to the little house, which I use as my library and study, and trotted back using a different track just as he had always done before, so that I willingly deluded myself into thinking that he was cured, and that there was now no reason for which he could not live another fifteen years—though, of course, I also knew that this was utter nonsense. My wife shared the delusion—*folie à deux*.

We also shared our delight in observing Ramses' little routines. For example, at home in England he would, once we were both out of bed (but not until then), jump through the cat-flap in our back door to the garden and race down the lawn to the bushes at the far end, rushing back and forth behind them, barking furiously at the dog on the other side of the tall and thick hedge dividing our garden from the one adjoining, the dog on the other side being his friend-enemy of whom neither he nor we ever caught so much as a glimpse. Incidentally, Ramses taught himself to use the cat-flap, which was already in the house when we moved in.

So regular was Ramses' habit that his route down the lawn was visible whether the grass was long or short. His path was indelibly imprinted on it and curiously was not a straight line but a very gentle curve. The garden was on two levels and sloped downwards; my wife and I would look down at the path in the grass with pleasure and almost with pride. Why the contemplation of such a slight thing gave us pleasure I cannot quite say: perhaps it gave us a false sense of security against the destructive workings of Time. We had already reached an age when any change would be for the worse.

When Ramses had had his little bark, lasting less than half a minute, he would return to the house, his duty done and his honour preserved. Once more, he had successfully defended his territory.

In fine weather, and when I was not working, I would lie down on the grass, read and go to sleep. Ramses would lie down beside me and go to sleep likewise, waking when I woke.

Ramses' restoration to health was of short duration. We were supposed to give him pills to control his heart failure, but this was not easy. Dogs do not like pills or medicines any more than do children. (I remember as a young child after my tonsillectomy—in those days performed on almost all middle class children—spitting out my medicine at the bottom of my hospital bed.) Ramses could detect a pill in his food, however cleverly we thought we had disguised it in something that he normally ate with relish, and was as capable of sifting the pill from it as any panner for gold was capable of sifting a flake of gold from mud and gravel. He would eat everything and leave the pill sitting pristine in his bowl. Liquid medicine he rejected, of course, because of its taste. My wife was very skilful at insinuating a pill down his throat so that he had no choice but to swallow it, but this was very unpleasant for him, and we feared to make him dislike or even fear us. That would have been even more painful to us than his death.

Even we could not disguise from ourselves the short-lived nature of his improvement. He had been attached to a drip in the veterinary clinic and it was by this means that the chemistry of his blood had been corrected, but the prolongation of his life by permanent attachment to a drip would have been impractical and cruel. We returned with him to England as we had planned.

We had sold our house as being far too large for our needs, a house that is now indissolubly linked in our minds to Ramses' residence there. We had bought a smaller house in a pleasant market town, and it was almost ready for us to move into. In the interim, we stayed with friends in a country house nearby, and it was there that Ramses entered the very last stage of his life. He was exhausted. If I tried to take him for a walk, he would stop after two or three yards and made it clear that he could not go on. I had to carry him to somewhere, under a tree, so that he could relieve himself.

But he still had all his mind, if that is not too grand a word for it. He was still able to scratch the door to inform us that he needed to go outside. By this time, he was eating and drinking very little, and was beyond temptation by the things that he had once liked. We discovered to our astonishment that there existed low-protein dog food for dogs in renal failure, but even by the standards of dog food it was unappetising, and Ramses would not eat a single mouthful of it. The vet had recommended it and also sold it to us, at great expense. I wondered whether any dog ever consented to eat it? After Ramses died, we donated the food to the PDSA for distribution to the dogs of the poor that were in renal failure.

In matters of food, Ramses was always highly discriminating. He was a canine *bon vivant*. Many people suppose that anything that a dog will eat is good enough for it, that for a dog, food is just fuel, but this was certainly not the case with Ramses. If we put two bowls side by side, one containing a little of what we had made for ourselves, and the other containing dog food (even that advertised as 'gourmet'), Ramses would invariably eat the first and leave the second. This was not a matter of mere imitation, a desire to do whatever we did, but of real aesthetic preference. A similar trial between 'gourmet' dog food and ordinary dog food produced a similar result. One does not enquire how sausages or politics are made, said Bismarck; *a fortiori* is this true of dog food, but the superior kind contained chicken, rabbit or beef, as well as indisputably recognisable vegetables.

Is the pampering of dogs, which I think is widespread, a manifestation of decadence, or of the breakdown of human relations that leads to the overinvestment in dogs of ever greater emotion, or is it, on the contrary, a sign of moral advance that one owes to one's dog the most pleasure that it is possible to give him? Is the increase in the life expectancy of dogs the result only of better veterinary care, or of the richer and fuller lives most dogs now have?

Is it wrong to concern oneself with the diet of a dog and expend money on it when there is so much poverty and hardship in the world? In relative terms, no doubt, there is much less poverty than there used to be, but in absolute terms there is quite enough to be getting on with. There is a school of moral philosophy that argues that we have a moral duty to use whatever wealth we have to produce the greatest reduction possible in human misery, and therefore that the expensive pampering of dogs is morally objectionable, indeed highly reprehensible. I think this is in fact a miserabilist philosophy, wrong in theory and disastrous in practice. Needless to say, care for dogs can go to absurd and even appalling extremes. I once saw an amusing but fundamentally serious Mexican film about a very rich widow who cares only for her small spoilt dog, a fluffy white Pomeranian (if my memory serves me, which experience teaches me that it might not). When the woman dies, her will directs that the dog should continue to live in precisely the same material conditions as before her death, being waited on hand and foot by the corps of servants in her vulgarly luxurious home. They hate the dog as a symbol of the frivolity of unearned wealth, an insult to their own poverty and hard lives, and conspire to poison the dog. The film is a mirror-image *Mumu*.

But the sensibility exactly opposite to that of the rich widow, namely that one has a duty to relieve with one's resources as much suffering as possible, is worse than merely ludicrous: it is destructive of all civilisation, all beauty, all enjoyment and, incidentally, much benevolence itself. Even theoretically it is absurd, for it supposes that all human suffering or happiness can be measured according to a single scale, which is obviously not true. And it would be horrible if one refused to help one's own neighbour, because one could use one's time and money to relieve much more suffering, say, the eradication of trachoma in a distant impoverished country.

Therefore, when I learn that my neighbour cooks regularly for her dog, I am amused but not appalled. Her husband likes to say that the dog eats better than he: but, of course, he is as besotted with the dog as his wife. The joke is a gentle one.

We could always tell how much Ramses enjoyed something by the number of times he licked his upper lip and jaw afterwards. If what he had just eaten was really good, he would want to capture the last molecule of it. Ever since, in the privacy of our own home, my wife and I have indicated the special deliciousness of something by imitating Ramses. Only dog owners speaking to other dog owners feel at ease in admitting such things. *They* will understand.

Ramses' taste for rich food once led him to be very naughty. We had eaten some tagliatelle in a cream and salmon sauce and there was some left over in the bowl. My wife had for separate reasons to leave the room and when *and I* we returned, the bowl was not only empty but sparklingly clean. We asked each other whether we had emptied it and washed the bowl, but neither of us had. Then my wife noticed a pawprint on the tablecloth, and all became clear. Unable to resist temptation, Ramses had jumped up on to the table and cleaned the bowl. We called him, and he came, creeping low on the ground. 'Look!' we said, pointing to the bowl, whereupon an unmistakable expression of guilt appeared on his face. He knew that he had done wrong.

But wrong in what sense? Morally wrong, or wrong in the sense that, empirically, it might lead to bad consequences for himself? But he must have known from experience that nothing bad that he did had any undesirable consequences for him, beyond a moment's stern voice and perhaps a wag of a finger, immediately after which he was completely forgiven. And, in fact, we were more amused or even proud of his exploit with the tagliatelle than angry. He had shown some initiative, and we were reassured that we had not so crushed his doggish nature that he was unable to take advantage of an opportunity when it presented itself. For form's sake we wagged our finger a little and he crouched yet lower on the ground. After all, we didn't want him to make a habit of it. But then we laughed and said 'Clever pig!' and Ramses understood at once that he had been forgiven. He ceased to crouch and waited to be picked up and cuddled. Both my wife and I being enthusiasts of Somerset Maugham's short stories, and one of the most famous of them being *Footprints in the Jungle*, we ever after referred to the episode as *Footprints on the Tablecloth*.

The day before Ramses died—as we shall see, a euphemistic way of saying the day before we had Ramses killed—I had had to go to London; I forget for what reason. When I returned in the evening, though he was ill, he still expressed his pleasure at seeing me. The next day, his fits of coughing were severe and we could do nothing to alleviate them. We took him out for a walk, which in reality meant carrying him out for what proved to be the last bowel motion of his life, under a very beautiful and ancient cedar tree. Later that evening, he had a very severe fit of coughing and we decided to take him to the vet as an emergency.

It was out of hours and the waiting toom was empty. Ramses, seemingly a little better, walked round the room with his usual intense curiosity. One might have thought then that there was nothing wrong with him: perhaps we were making a fuss over nothing, perhaps he might live a good while yet. At the same time, we knew this could not be.

We told the vet—a young woman of polite but professional manner—of his coughing fits. She examined him and pronounced him in severe heart failure. His coughing fits would only worsen and cause him great distress.

'It is up to you, of course,' she said, 'but perhaps the time is come…'

She left the room for us to decide. Somehow, she made it clear that she did not expect our decision to take long and would not have remained long on the premises if it did. I had the perhaps unworthy thought that her main concern was that she should not be called again later in the night.

Our discussion was brief and painful. With Ramses on our lap, we spoke of his imminent death whatever we decided. We knew that we must make our heads prevail over our hearts, always difficult to do, and exclude from our minds the thought that perhaps the vet was wrong. We made the decision which I can hardly bear to name and called the vet back into the room.

She prepared the necessary equipment, a syringe and an ampoule. What a banal end to a life of passionate engagement with the world, as Ramses' had been! My wife wanted him to die with him on her lap, she who had never known all those years ago how attached one could become to a dog. As the vet raised the needle a priest raises the chalice, having first drawn up the fatal liquid, we said 'Goodbye, Piggy,' words as inadequate to our feelings as any ever uttered.

When the vet put the needle into Ramses' front leg, he gave a little jump, not more. He did not snarl, for we were with him, so what harm could come to him? I hoped against hope that the vet would find no vein in his leg, not of course in the hope that she would have to try to find another one, but in the hope that she would call the whole thing off as having been a terrible mistake. But the vet, with a skill that I could admire but not be grateful for, found a vein at once and drew back a little blood into the syringe to establish the fact.

My next hope was that the drug would not work: but of course it did. Ramses closed his eyes, stopped breathing and lost control of his bladder. My wife, who normally would have disliked this very much, did not complain. We thanked the vet, paid and left.

We moved with heavy hearts that evening into our new house (actually three hundred years old). We had taken Ramses to see it in his last days, for we did not wish to live where there was no association with him at all: and indeed, he had managed despite all to inspect the house as if he were going to live there and make it his own, even climbing one of the flights of quite steep stairs.

We slept that night near Ramses'in his body basket, which was on my wife's side of the bed. I woke several times in the night and went to look at him in the basket. Absurd though I knew it to be, I hoped against hope that it had been a bad dream, that Ramses was still alive and that he would greet me as usual, but *rigor mortis* had set in. Death was indeed death.

From the first, I experienced guilt at having brought it about, indeed having commanded it: I who should have been his protector was his killer! The fact that I acted from the best of intentions, to prevent his further, increasing distress, did not console me as it should have done, had I been a thoroughgoing and convinced utilitarian. But I was not, and still am not. It is always difficult, if not impossible, to align one's thoughts with one's emotions, a difficulty (or impossibility) brilliantly described in John Stuart Mill's *Autobiography*. He has a crisis in which he questions himself:

> Suppose that all your objects in life were realized; that all the changes in institutions and opinions which you were looking forward to, could be completely effected at this very instant: would this be a great joy and happiness to you? And an irrepressible self-consciousness distinctly answered 'No!' At this my heart sank within me: the whole foundation on which my life was constructed fell down. All my happiness was to have been found in my continual pursuit of this end. The end had ceased to charm. And how could there ever again be any interest in the means?

When I tell myself that Ramses had very little time left in any case, whatever we had decided, and that such time would have been filled with suffering, and that all this was the most evident truth, my sense of guilt persisted as strongly as ever.   human

What, then, of euthanasia? I see the arguments in favour and I see the arguments against. For myself, I would want it and I know that, in effect, it is already practised, though in a disguised and no doubt hypocritical fashion. I do not mean any criticism by these terms, *disguised* and *hypocritical*, for I do not believe that life would be tolerable without disguise and hypocrisy; without them we should live in perfectly transparent houses, which would be a nightmare both for the watched and the watchers (but especially for the former). But while I should like the benefits of euthanasia myself—I mean the *possibility* of euthanasia, I don't, at the moment, mind living a little longer—I fear it for others, especially under the present regime of medical care in Britain.

I remember a manager in the hospital in which I worked prowling the wards, seeking patients supposedly fit for discharge, not of course for their own benefit but in pursuit of a target set by the government, namely that patients arriving in the hospital in need of a bed should not have to wait more than four hours before one was found—there being financial penalties for the hospital if the target were not met. The manager in question had no medical qualifications whatever, and though as an individual he was pleasant enough and far from stupid, and though for the moment he confined himself to *asking* doctors whether their patients could not safely be discharged, it was certainly not beyond powers of human imagination to envisage a time when such a figure might demand—for the good of society—that old people who were spending too long a time in hospital beds should be shuffled off this mortal coil to make room for others. Certainly, when I asked hospital managers what was the order that they would refuse to obey, they failed to see the meaning of the question: their careers depended upon obeying orders (as do most careers, to a greater or lesser extent), and they found their orders worthy of obedience even when manifestly stupid, absurd or against the interests of patients. Increasingly, the same tendency is found in the medical profession itself, inexorably leading not to voluntary, but compulsory, euthanasia, and not necessarily for benefit of the human beings to be put down, to borrow the veterinary term for it.

When I say or write that Ramses *died*, I feel a stab of conscience, not merely for what I did, or caused to be done, but because of the employment of a euphemism by which I seek to minimise my part in his end. This is bad faith on my part, avoiding my responsibility.

I am reminded of the death of my mother. She did not have to die, at least not when she did: she starved herself nearly to death after an operation. (Here, truly, was a case of the operation having been a success but the patient nevertheless having died.) Her death was lingering; it took five weeks and was an unhappy end to an unhappy life. Towards the very end, she fell unconscious but showed signs of agitation as if of suffering.

The young doctor, a few years into his career, asked me (knowing that I, too, was a doctor) whether he could sedate her to reduce her agitation. I knew what he really meant. I agreed to his proposal which after a short while had the unspoken effect. I think we were grateful, the young doctor and I, that neither of us had been explicit: we preferred to keep our innermost thoughts to, and perhaps from, ourselves.

In the morning, it was time to bury Ramses, his death having proved overnight to have been no bad dream. (I took a photograph of him on his deathbed, which my wife

then threw away or hid as morbid and distressing.) Our
first task was to find a stone slab to place over his grave.
We went to a large do-it-yourself depot where, even quite
early in the morning, an army of tinkerers were already in
search of materials to beautify, or further enkitsch, their
homes. How different was our search from theirs! How
shallow seemed their concerns to us, how callous their indifference to our distress! Absurd, of course: in any crowd,
there will always be a secret mourner to whose recent loss
we show a seemingly callous indifference.

We chose a slab–the right shape, size and colour—and
returned home. Then I dug a grave, the first I had ever dug,
in a flowerbed in our small back garden. In it, we placed
Ramses in his basket, on his favourite cloth, with his favourite toy, one of his little red leather harnesses, a lead,
and even a pack of 'gourmet' dog food. It occurred to me
that if, some hundreds of years hence, archaeologists dug
in our garden, they would come to the conclusion that
there had existed a primitive civilisation at the site whose
population (poor benighted fools!) had worshipped their
dogs, believing in their afterlife, for they buried them with
all that was necessary to tide them over until they reached
the canine heaven. With what excitement would they pub-
lish their findings, so unexpected given the matter-of-fact
remains of the same date—plastic bottles, computer ca-
bles, etc.—hitherto excavated in the area.

Within a few weeks, we went again to North Wales, to
order a black slate headstone in the shape of a gothic arch,
with the following simple inscription

RAMSES

1992 – 2007

in an elegant font. I made the aesthetic mistake of order-
ing the lettering of the inscription too large, but even so, it
was more elegant a tombstone than the majority of tomb-

stones today, which are made of the glossily polished stone also used for kitchen islands and inscribed with demotic abbreviations and shallow messages, such as 'Good night, sleep tight, Dad'.

On collecting the tombstone, we returned to Aberdaron beach, where we gathered pebbles of many different colours to put in a small bowl beside Ramses' tomb. This had a secret meaning whose opacity, except to us, made it precious.

All these years later, we still sometimes put flowers on his grave, and have planted an olive tree in his memory in our land in France, also with a Welsh slate plaque. And when we place flowers on his grave, we speak to him as if he could still hear (and, of course, still understand) us.

That we should have had to bury Ramses on the first full day of our residence in our new home might have been considered as an ill augury, but, on the contrary, it proved to be a consolation to us. He is still near to us, in some faint type of presence. I should add, before anyone thinks that I am a believer in the transmigration of souls, or anything like that, that I am a materialist at least in the sense of believing that no mental activity persists after the material dissolution of our brains (which, after all, is why death is a tragedy), though at the same time I believe that our mentation will never be explicable in the language of physiology or chemistry and that we shall always remain mysterious to ourselves—as I fervently hope. No, I am simply trying to record my thoughts and emotions as they were and are, without claiming that they reflect or reveal any other reality, and acknowledging also that they are not consistent with my philosophical beliefs.

Thus, when I say that my wife and I stop at locations associated in our minds with him, such as the place in remote country roads where we had a picnic with him, or where we let him relieve himself, I do not claim that some ghostly emanation remains of him there. Rather, it is a way of recapturing moments of happiness, inevitably now gone forever but for which we were still grateful, even if our gratitude is now strongly admixed with pain:

> That is the land of lost content,
> I see it shining plain:
> The happy highways where I went,
> And cannot come again.

Immediately after his death, I looked for his pawprints wherever he had been in the last days before his death, but of course found none. I was like the widow who searched for her husband after his death, the marriage having lasted many years, though I did not go as far as to hallucinate, as some widows do, the presence of the deceased.

One of the places I looked for him particularly (and with particular absurdity) was on a spur of sand in the stream—a torrent in the rains—that passes through our land in France. It was from this spur that Ramses launched himself, gingerly at first, into the stream, first dipping a paw delicately into it. He would walk a few steps in the stream, distracted sometimes by dragonflies, and then return to shore.

I would visit that spur, about three hundred yards from the house, every time we returned to the house. Heavy rains washed it away one day, and though it later re-formed, it was never again the same for me: it was no longer the sand on which the paws of Ramses had trod.

The strength of our attachment to Ramses, which was very quick to develop, made me more tolerant of the foibles and absurdities of others, for I knew that others would find our attachment excessive, absurd, even pathological, and I desired their indulgence. Reason, said Hume, is the slave of the passions, and no one can be argued out of his affections by being shown that logically or empirically they are ridiculous, or that the object of them is unworthy of them.

In my youth, when I thought myself clever, I was not so much offended by what I thought were absurd beliefs, but vain enough to believe that I could argue others out of them. Thus, when two missionaries from the Jehovah's Witnesses came to the door (they never came singly), I would engage them in discussion and confound them. This was not very difficult because, on the whole, they were good people rather than clever, and logic was not their strong point: rather, their evident kindness and their happiness in their belief were their strong points. If, as was fortunately impossible, I had been able to argue them out of their beliefs, it would have destroyed their contentment for no reason other than to satisfy my ego. My impulse to argue with them was not fundamentally different from that of a small boy who picks the legs and wings off a fly.

To examine oneself without the distorting lens of some psychological theory is to become more tolerant, for one discovers just how difficult the mastery of one's own foibles is, and that one is not a rational creature even where rationality should be sovereign. I have already, elsewhere, told the story of a bookseller who was a devotee of the Albanian communist dictator, Enver Hoxha. He was much disappointed by the fact that his few customers were much more interested in Bibles than in the memoirs of his hero, whose one indisputable literary talent was for invective and abuse. (He spared only Stalin, whom he worshipped.) He, the bookseller, had bought a whole collection of books from a spiritualist who had passed over to the other side, many of the books published by the Psychic Book Club in the 1940s along normal book club lines. I have long planned to visit the address of the former owner of these books, a lower middle-class neighbourhood where net curtains would once have twitched on the arrival of a visitor, and where no doubt seances were held in darkened rooms...

Among the books was one that included the best technique for getting in touch with the spirit of your departed dog. The book was complete with photographs of ghostly canine revenants, recalled to earth by spirit mediums. Such photographs, surely, could only have been the product of fraud, or at least of fabrication, though fraud and fabrication are not quite the same, insofar as the fabricator might believe that he is acting in the interests of spreading a truth in which he genuinely believes, but which regrettably is lacking other tangible evidence. (This is far from unknown in science. Fabricators manipulate results to coincide with a theory that they strongly believe to be true. Perhaps such people are more dangerous than outright frauds, whose flamboyance is often their downfall.)

I laughed at these photographs, of course, but there was something melancholy, sad, even tragic about the book, especially considering the date of its publication, 1940, the year following the great slaughter of dogs in 1939 at the outset of the war, when it was feared that there would not be enough food to feed them. A quarter of a million were put down, almost certainly to the great grief of the overwhelming majority of their owners. If it had not been for the destruction and slaughter to follow, this episode would be remembered as one of the greatest causes of misery of the time, but it was soon forgotten among the bombs.

If people in 1939 were as attached to their dogs as we are to ours, what a quantity of suffering must have resulted! In such circumstances, it was only to be expected that some among them should find consolation, and perhaps absolution, in imagining that the dogs to whose death they had consented were in some sense still living. At least they did no harm to others in believing this, and I am in no position to mock them, I who talk to Ramses over his grave, and sometimes at other times too, though I have no belief at all in an afterlife.

Is grief over the death of an animal ludicrous, and if it is not, at what point in the evolutionary scale does it become so? People keep all kinds of pets and grow fond even of those incapable of reciprocation. I am far from denying that my love for Ramses was excessive, but such an admission does not alter the facts. I read with a certain dismay the book by Emmanuel Carrère, *The Adversary*, which tells the story of a man who, to avoid the humiliation of having to admit to his parents, who had placed all their hope in him, that he had failed his exams early on in medical school, pretending on the contrary to have passed them, and continuing the pretence for decades, to the extent of having a job at the World Health Organization in Geneva. His wife, his children, his parents and parents-in-law believed him, but when exposure of his lies became inevitable, he killed them all (his father-in-law having previously died in a mysterious fall down the stairs when only the protagonist was present).

At his trial, the accused exhibited no emotion concerning their deaths, but when asked to recall his childhood, he broke down inconsolably at the memory of his dog. Reading this, I could not help but wonder whether I suffered from a form, highly attenuated of course, of this pathology?

Is this pathology, supposing it to exist,[6] a matter of in-

---

6 Adolf Hitler was another emotional cripple, seemingly capable of

dividual psychology alone, or is there a social or cultural dimension to it? I know a few people who said they could never have another dog because they could never again go through the grief of losing one, but who would cheerfully admit that in the event of being widowed, they would have no qualms about remarrying, and indeed in some cases have done so. There are no new things under the sun, at least where human behaviour is concerned: the only question is whether this kind of reaction is more common than it once was, and if so, what the increase signifies.

I don't suppose a definite or definitive answer can be given to the question, but I should not be surprised if attachment to dogs is deeper and more all-consuming than ever before. More people live in single-person households than ever before, and it seems that human relations are more unstable also. Perhaps the ever-more extravagant accoutrements available for dogs might merely be part of a general trend to extend choice in order to keep consumers buying and the wheels of commerce turning. Still, the fact that there is now an immense range of dog foods available, whereas sixty years ago there were only two or three brands (and even they were a comparatively recent innovation), suggests that people are extending consumerism to their dogs. From this trend, we—my wife and I—were not immune, and the very fact that we observed Ramses' preferences so closely, and acted upon them, demonstrates it.

Occasionally, in the prison in which I worked there would be a prisoner who had been found guilty of cruelty to a dog. If the nature of his crime became known to the general prison population, as almost always it would, such a prisoner had to ask for special protection, in the same

---

expressing deep affection only for dogs.

way as sex offenders. Without this protection, he would be set upon by the other prisoners and beaten. A murderer who had, say, strangled his girlfriend to death in a fit of jealousy or a man who had shot a shopkeeper during a robbery[7] required no such protection. On the prisoners' scale of values, then, cruelty to a dog was of a different order of wrongfulness from that of a murder (except of a child). Anyone might murder in the right, or rather, wrong, circumstances, but cruelty to a dog is indicative of an irredeemably bad character.

I could almost sympathise with this point of view. It is easier to think of mitigating circumstances for a murder than for cruelty to a dog, at least cruelty of a persistent kind. Some murders, at least, are the result of a sudden loss of control after repeated insults or ill-treatment. Most of the murders in which I was an expert witness were not of this kind, but at least one was, and though of course the murder was still very wrong, yet I felt some sympathy for the perpetrator. But it requires a very bad character, which the aforementioned murderer did not have, to be persistently cruel to a dog.

What I do not know is whether prisoners a century ago, imprisoned for cruelty to a dog (I presume there were a few, for the notion of such cruelty as a crime had already developed), would have been the object of other prisoners' righteous anger. If they were not, it would suggest either that prisoners had since undergone a process of emotional refinement with regard to attitude to dogs, or of an increasing callousness towards their fellow humans. Another interpretation is possible: prison discipline has

---

7　Now typically described by police spokesmen as 'a robbery that went tragically wrong', as if the happy outcome would have left the shopkeeper in possession of his life and the robber in possession of the shopkeeper's goods.

slackened to the point that it is now easier for prisoners to attack other prisoners whom they disfavour.

The year after Ramses died (that phrase again!), my wife and I went for the first time in our lives to Crufts, the annual dog show that is said to be the largest such show in the world. I thought we should enjoy it and that it would make an interesting article, but neither of these hopes was fulfilled. On the contrary, we disliked it quite strongly, and felt at once on admission that there was something profoundly wrong with it.

The merchants of products for dogs—or more accurately, for the owners of dogs—were there in force, as one might expect. They stimulated my inner censoriousness, never far below the surface, for their displays seemed to me indicative of a decadent society, at a loss to know what to do next and, in its exhaustion, avid for novelty. I have already confessed to having been prepared to spend freely on Ramses' veterinary care, and expressed my sympathy for a man of modest means who used his financial substance in this way; but even I drew a limit well before diamond-studded collars for dogs, or the other jewelled accessories for dogs that we saw on sale at Crufts. Was my disgust mere envy, that diamond-studded collars were beyond my means, and likely to remain so, or were there other, better reasons for it?

The diamond-studded collars were flashy and vulgar, and not at all elegant. They were in the vilest taste, but vile taste is commonplace, and anyone who reacts too strongly to it will soon die of apoplexy. No; there was something else wrong with them.

The dog with a diamond-studded collar is being used as an extension of, and advertisement for, his owner. Not *look at the dog*, but *look at me and what I can afford*, is the message. And that is what is wrong with Crufts: the word *show* in dog-show is indicative. We loved Ramses for himself, not for the admiration that we should attract to ourselves for possessing so pleasing a dog, however proud we were when he did, in fact, please.

The dogs at Crufts were beautiful, sleek and groomed to perfection to be the very best of their breeds—even the breeds that I find the least attractive, those of toughs, pimps and idlers. But to see forty perfect examples of any breed in an arena, English sheepdogs, for example, beautiful as each of them might be, is not to increase but decrease one's regard for dogs. What we loved in Ramses was his strong personality, his individuality, his determination, his self-chosen little habits, his obstinacy, his unpredictability, his passionate engagement with the world around him: and here were dogs reduced to the status of clones, whose minor variations their owners did their best to iron out, so that they might reach some arbitrary ideal of perfection for their breed. It was to treat the dogs as objects rather than as subjects; and when I saw the judges, obviously very learned in their way, specialised in one breed or another, look into a dog's mouth, or lift its leg, or measure its tail, examine the length of its coat, and so forth, I was—horrified or disgusted would be too strong words, or at least not quite accurate—saddened. The dogs were being used as a means to glorify their owners, a glory that was of a very peculiar type inasmuch as it was discernible or comprehensible only to those with a similar, and to my mind, perverted, scale of values.

We all live in what might be called a microclimate of virtues—a philatelist, for example, sees all kinds of virtues or defects in a stamp that escape non-philatelists entirely, and grows excited over such minutiae as the number of perforations, whose importance would mystify anyone else—but, to continue with the example, a postage stamp is an inanimate object, the passion for it being entirely unidirectional.

The dogs at Crufts were put through their paces under the critical eyes of the judges. Of course, these paces were adapted to the breed: you can't expect a dachshund to do what a greyhound can do. But all the dogs of any given breed were expected to do precisely the same as others of their breed, only with more precision, according to some pre-arranged programme or routine, as far as I could see arbitrary, useless and humiliating The whole thing struck me as a canine *Brave New World*.

When a dog stumbled in its performance, or for some reason refused to go on with it, it was a disaster for its owner, who saw in this the end of all his hopes for a prize. The judges, apparently, were severe and unforgiving. The slightest physical deviation from the criteria by which a dog was judged, the slightest manifestation of independent will, and the dog was eliminated from consideration for a prize. Though one of Ramses' grandparents had won a prize at Crufts, or so we were told, the thought of putting him through the grooming and training necessary even for entry to the competition appalled us. To show, or show off, a dog is not a good reason for keeping one, and turns a highly sentient being into the equivalent of a very expensive handbag with a fashionable manufacturer's logo displayed conspicuously on it, valued not for itself but for its effect on others and admired for its cost, rather than its use or even beauty. The immense amount of labour that went into the production of these canine clones and robots put me in mind of what the Marquis de Custine wrote about a splendid military parade that turned thousands of men into seeming automata, in the reign of Nicholas I in Russia: thus, says Custine, do tyrannies demand prodigious efforts to bring forth trifles. Crufts consisted essentially of trifles brought about by tyranny.

And yet, at the same time I cannot honestly say that I am never impressed by a military parade carried out to perfection. Whether that impression is one of admiration or horror depends on the context, social and political. The Trooping of the Colour, for example, does not horrify me as a Soviet military parade did. And with regard to Ramses, the fact is that he was the product, if I may use so impersonal a term about a unique individual, of a long and artificial process of selection to bring about precisely the features that he had. The books say that he was bred to chase rats, his small size enabling him to pursue them into confined spaces into which they retreated, though whether this is true history or mere fable I do not know. No one had a blueprint for a Yorkshire Terrier in mind as he chose to interbreed dogs of rat-catching abilities, but a Yorkshire Terrier was what emerged after generations of breeding dogs for such abilities. And certainly, the books devoted to the characteristics of different breeds of dog mention that Yorkshire Terriers like to be involved in all that their keepers do, that they want to be with them all the time, and that they are inquisitive by nature, all of which was true of Ramses, true to the nth degree as it were.

Ramses, then, was the result of a long eugenic process, though how many generations it would take to turn a wolf into a Yorkshire Terrier I do not know. That Ramses was in some sense 'artificial', the product of human intention rather than of an unaided 'natural' process, was no doubt true. No one, however, had had a Platonic form of Yorkshire Terrier in mind in advance when the breed was bred, so it would be interesting to know (and perhaps it is known) at what point people said, 'We now have the very breed we desire, so we shall develop it no further.' And what can be brought about artificially can be extinguished artificially. I read recently that Yorkshire Terriers have fallen out of favour with the public (in favour of lesser breeds without the charm) to such an extent that they might not survive as a breed. I think the world would be impoverished—not by very much, perhaps, but by a little—if they did not survive because of the whims of fashion.

The fact that Ramses was not a purely natural being, except in the vacuous sense that everything that exists is natural, that he was 'artificial', did not alter our affection for him in the slightest. The fact that he had been bred to be affectionate did not change the fact that he *was* affectionate: and, as Bishop Butler says, every thing is what it is and not another thing. We do not say of an intelligent person that, since he was born of intelligent parents, he is not really intelligent, but only pretending to be, or artificially, so. It was sufficient for us that Ramses delighted us.

Because we inherited him from a friend, we did not know how expensive pure-bred dogs are. They are objects of commerce, and where there is commerce there is theft. I did not realise until quite late in his life that he had to be protected not only from mange and kennel cough and worms and ticks, but from thieves. I do not count myself as naïve when it comes to the repertoire of human wickedness—I have travelled into murderous civil wars and worked in a prison, after all—but it had not occurred to me that people might steal dogs to order. To steal a dog is an act of deep-dyed villainy, for the thief almost certainly knows the grief his theft will cause but goes ahead and commits it anyway, his thirst for gain trumping his human feeling.

Oddly enough, it did not occur to me immediately that a prize at Crufts was not only a source of pride to a breeder, but of money. Commerce makes the world go round and, as Montesquieu said, it softens the manners of those who engage in it, at least sometimes (compare the manners of NHS and private practice receptionists, for example, the one grating and the other unctuous), but it can also call forth the evil that always lurks in the human heart.

It was at Crufts that I met the only veterinary forensic toxicologist in the country (or so I was told). His presence was necessary, because some breeders were prepared to drug or poison their competitors' dogs. Sedation would ruin a dog's performance in the obedience trials, and a good dose of diarrhoea would place him *hors de combat* and probably cause him to be expelled altogether from the show for fear that he might infect the other dogs in what must be one of densest, albeit temporary, dog populations in the world. So far, the toxicologist told me, there had been no poisonings that year: but his very presence discouraged them, for it made discovery much more likely. Most years, however, there were nevertheless some poisonings.

How could anyone who loved dogs poison them? To adapt Lovelace's poem slightly, the answer might be:

I could not kill the dog, my dear,
Loved I not money more.

But on the train home from Crufts, I discovered that not everyone in the dog industry, if I may so call it, loves dogs. I sat opposite a man who was reading a dog magazine, and dogs being the best social icebreakers, at least in England, we started to talk. He was a large-scale breeder: at least, he said that he was.

'I suppose,' I said, in the knowledge that what I was saying was completely banal, 'that you love dogs.'

'Not at all,' he replied. 'For me it is just a business, a way of making money.'

My blood ran cold. I suspect that he enjoyed the shock that he produced in me. I also suspect that he was not trying to disguise the strength of his affection for dogs, as very emotional people sometimes do, but that he was stating a plain and simple truth.

Our conversation ended there and then. (Perhaps as he intended, he didn't want to speak to yet another dog-bore delivering himself of a dithyramb to dogs.) I noticed that he was examining a page in his magazine as a second-hand car dealer might examine a list of prices in a car magazine. His eye was purely rational, that of a Gradgrind among dog-breeders.

Not everyone at Crufts was exploitative or treated dogs as a means to a financial end, however. We met an Israeli woman living in London who was showing her Dobermanns, a breed that I have always associated with aggression. Indeed, Dobermanns had first been bred up by a German tax-collector, Herr Dobermann, in the days when taxes were collected door-to-door. Not everyone was pleased to see Herr Dobermann, so he developed his breed to protect him and to encourage disgorgement of the sums required. (How long did it take?) Presumably, this use of dogs would find favour with orthodox Moslems, but these particular Dobermanns were as cooing doves, sleek and handsome. They loved their mother.

The owner of the Dobermanns told us that she had been so besotted by her dogs that one day her husband came to her and said that she would have to choose between him and the dogs.

'I didn't hesitate for a moment,' she said. 'I told him to go.' She hadn't regretted it for a moment. 'Whenever I feel broody,' she continued, being still of child-bearing age, 'I breed some more Dobermanns.'

Though her love for her dogs was evident, our opinion of the show was unchanged.

After Ramses' death—after we had him killed—I could not easily put aside my guilt, even though I knew that he could not have survived much longer in any case. Under English law, even to shorten life deliberately by five minutes is murder, and rightly so (I am not here speaking of the contested question of voluntary euthanasia): anything else would lead to a slippery slope down which might slip many an elderly person with an estate to leave. And while I do not make the law my only moral compass—as do those who say 'There's no law against it!' when criticised for having done something wrong—in this instance, I think the law is right.

My guilt was rekindled when, years later, my wife and I met Madame Jacquelynne in the street in Paris where we stay when we are there. A very old lady who walks with difficulty, Madame Jacquelynne, has a very old dog, Julie, who is by no means pretty, being a spontaneous mixture of aesthetically incompatible breeds, but she is seventeen years old and while not frisky, exactly, is still in good health. We remarked that Julie seemed to be scrupulous about urinating in the gutter, to which Madame Jacquelynne replied, 'She's the cleanest in the *quartier*,' though whether she meant cleanest of dogs, or cleanest of dogs *and* men in the *quartier* we were not quite sure. At any rate, we had the impression that Jacquelynne and Julie lived for one another.

Perhaps Ramses could have lived another two years if we had done more for him? Perhaps, if we had been more attentive, his illness would not have developed as it did? Guilt reviews the past as a public prosecutor goes through the papers in a case. Is there anyone's life—any period of anyone's life—in which a prosecuting conscience could not find cause for guilt? We frequently recalled the occasions on which we were not as good to Ramses as we should or might have been, and even caused him unhappiness: that is to say, unhappiness that we could easily have avoided causing him. I do not include our daily departure for work in this category.

Once in our house in France, for example, my wife and I had a furious row. I cannot remember what it was about, but I know from experience of all subsequent rows (not very many, I hasten to add) that it was about nothing at all. (Of course, psychoanalysts would not agree. Adapting Lear's angry response to Cordelia, that nothing will come of nothing, they would say that no argument about nothing is about nothing.) Ramses disliked it almost as much when we had rows as when there were thunderstorms, though he reacted in a different way to them: not by agitation or by climbing the walls, but by slinking away miserably and hiding himself, emerging only when the row had been over for a few minutes.

On this occasion, the row was unusually terrible. The isolation of our house encouraged an excess both as to volume and content, or rather discouraged inhibition, for there was no one to overhear us (apart from Ramses). This in itself suggests that even at the height of temper some self-control remains: we wouldn't have shouted as we did if there had been neighbours to hear. People vary in their ability to control themselves according to their natural temperaments, the legal dispensation under which they live and their social circumstances.

There must have been a lull in the course of our argument, for suddenly we heard Ramses barking plaintively from a distance. We stopped arguing at once, and we went in search of Ramses in what we thought was the direction of his bark. My wife found him, poor dog, wet and bedraggled and standing on a rock in the middle of the stream a few hundred yards away to which he had fled in his fright, and from which he was now unable to return. She rescued him and brought him back to the house, where we dried him in a towel. Our argument was over, and the ease with which we stopped it was testimony to its triviality in the first place. The suffering we had inflicted on Ramses shamed us into reconciliation: a dog is a very good marriage counsellor.

Although I did not myself see Ramses on his rock, shivering and frightened, the image of him there in my mind is as vivid as any actual memory. This tells us that vividness is not veracity, which is why testimony may be false without being mendacious. To rehearse a scene in one's imagination is to turn it into a memory, one of the reasons (but only one) why speed is an element of justice.

What fools we felt to have expended so much passion over nothing! Humiliated by our own stupidity, we had a motive to forget what the argument had been about.

As for Ramses, he forgave us at once. I am not sure that his forgiveness was mere forgetfulness, for he was by no means forgetful. For example, he met my brother only twice in his life, at an interval of some years. He had taken to him at once, and when my brother arrived at our front door the second time, Ramses' reaction even before we opened it was that to someone whom he recognised and liked, quite different from his reaction to a complete stranger arriving for the first time. I suspect, though luckily I had no empirical evidence of this, that he would have shied away from anyone who had once been deliberately cruel to him. Thus, I concluded that he extended his forgiveness to us because he understood our feelings of benevolence towards him: for it was to us that he turned in his distress, even though it was we who had caused his distress in the first place. I can still hear his plaintive barking in my mind's ear, and it still causes me pain in the heart.

Quite early in our life with Ramses, he ran out of the front door when we opened it to a taxi that was to take us to a restaurant. We never allowed him out on the street on his own or without a lead, which I suppose he must have experienced as an unjustified restriction of his freedom. As it happened, we had some friends who had lost their dog, a Jack Russell called Ted, when he rushed from the front door as Ramses had done. Ted had run straight in front of a car and been killed instantly, to the horror and grief of our friends, who as a result never felt able to have another dog. Moreover, Ramses' predecessor in the household from which we inherited him was a Yorkshire Terrier called Horus who had been killed in the same way.[8]

Our road, fortunately, was quiet and without much traffic, but it led by another road of a few hundred yards to a very busy thoroughfare. My wife rushed out after Ramses, calling on him angrily to come back. But Ramses ran on ahead, then stopped, looking back almost long enough for my wife to catch up with him, and then running on ahead again. I could have sworn that Ramses had a teasing expression on his face, that he was enjoying himself, almost laughing. But as if by some instinct, that of an adolescent testing the limits, he let himself be caught before he reached the busy thoroughfare, and my wife, by now out of breath and furious, brought him back by the scruff of his

---

8 As, incidentally, was Mao, the protagonist of the book, *La Mort de Mao*. The author remarks on the habit of giving dogs the name of eminent personages, and says that it is by no means a sign of disrespect, rather the reverse. But Jules Roy was no Maoist: he had simply just returned from a visit to China when he first had Mao, his dog.

neck. Ramses never ran from the front door again, perhaps because we were more vigilant when opening it in his presence, and perhaps because he had learned his lesson.

He was once hit by a car, however. I was walking him in London, where we were living for a short time. It was on one of those leads which extends if the dog pulls, unless it is locked by the person holding it. All dogs pull on their leads, because it is in their nature to walk faster than humans; and every human also pulls on the lead when his dog wants to linger too long over a smell at the bottom of a tree or lamppost. It is amusing to see a dog pull on a lead, eager to reach a destination unknown to its master, but not so amusing to see a master pull a dog on its lead. The necessity to keep dogs under restraint for much of their lives is one of the arguments of those who believe that the keeping of dogs as household pets is inherently cruel and demeaning to them.

Anyhow, while walking Ramses in our street in London, I let him extend the lead too far and he reached the kerb on the roadside, where a passing car struck him a glancing blow. The sound and sensation of the car hitting him were horrible and very distinctive, and I can still conjure them in my memory. Fortunately, Ramses was not injured or maimed in any way; he simply rolled over, a little surprised perhaps, and got up to continue his walk as if nothing had happened. I imagined having to return home to my wife to tell her that Ramses had been killed in a car accident, while he was supposed to be under my control. I had my excuses ready: yes, it was my fault, but anyone can have momentary lapses of concentration, the whole episode lasted only a second or two. The dullest mind works like a flash and is brilliantly inventive when it comes to making excuses for its possessor. The faculty of excusing oneself is infinite in its reach.

We were not perfect carers for Ramses, even if we loved him more than was reasonable—if love can ever be measured by reason.

If our love was not quite at first sight, it did not take long to develop. At first, Ramses slept downstairs in his basket. He was allowed into our bedroom with the first coffee of the morning, when he fairly flew on to the bed. We were as pleased to seem him as he was to see us. We would call to him, 'Are you coming, Piggy?', whereupon he would gallop up the uncarpeted stairs, his little claws making a pleasant clicking sound on the wood.

Then we made a new rule: if either of us was ill, Ramses could sleep all night in the bedroom in his basket at the foot of the bed. We weren't ill very often, of course, in fact very rarely, but it did not take many relaxations of the rules before Ramses was sleeping on our bed every night. What started as a privilege—on both sides—became a right. We have since discovered that this progression is by no means a rare one among dog owners—or in society in general.

Once, when we had to go away for a week and could find no one to look after Ramses, we employed a couple through an agency to stay the week in our house and look after him. They were an elderly couple from Northumberland, retired teachers, who now spent their lives in this fashion, going from house to house to look after dogs for a time. I almost envied them. I could think of few more pleasant occupations, interesting without being onerous; I should imagine that the great majority of people able and prepared to employ them were decent, kindly and trusting. And indeed, one knew at first meeting that they were trustworthy; Ramses took to them at once, which was a good, indeed the best possible, sign. I think that if we had left a million gold coins in a room, they would still have been there when we returned, for their honesty was a matter of character rather than of prudence. In any case, even if we had been wrong, it is, as Doctor Johnson said, better sometimes to be deceived than never to trust.

The couple told us, on our return, that when it was time to go to bed, they went upstairs preceded by Ramses who, on the first floor, turned left into our bedroom as a matter of course or right, and jumped onto our bed to sleep, while they climbed to the floor above where was their bedroom. We heard the story with pleasure.

How did Ramses worm his way into our affections so easily, quickly and deeply? I had originally thought to read some of the immense academic literature on dogs before embarking on this memoir, and accumulated a small library of books to this end, but decided against extensive reading. This was for two reasons, the first being that I did not want to provide 'real', which is to say mechanical, explanations for experiences and phenomena that delighted me, and that would cause that delight to evaporate as I wrote. A behaviourist might, for example, explain Ramses' affection for us by reference to stimulus and response, making of him the canine equivalent of *Homo oeconomicus*, that is to say the *Canis oeconomicus*. In other words, according to theorists, every thing is not, *pace* Bishop Butler, what it is but really something else entirely.

Another theory would be that dogs have been selected to show affection for humans, and this in some way detracts from the reality of that reflection, because it is not truly chosen. We have made of dogs self-fulfilling prophecies, and indeed we choose the dog with the kind of character that we want. This is not quite true of Ramses, who was almost thrust upon us by circumstances, but it is true nonetheless that we have bred dogs more efficiently to parasitise us. But so what?

The second reason I did not consult my books was geographical: my books were in England and I was in France, all but confined to a flat in Paris. I had long contemplated writing a memoir of Ramses, straight after his death, in fact, before my thoughts and feelings had sedimented, so to speak, but other projects and demands on my time got in the way for thirteen years. But suddenly I had no further excuse; it was now or never.

I shall now read the books *after* I have completed my little memoir, not before. I look forward to reading the slim volume with my favourite title: *Why Bad Dogs?* The answer, of course, is that there is no such thing as a bad dog: there are only bad, or ignorant, or foolish, dog owners. Dogs were born without Original Sin, and therefore must be brought up to be bad. The question then becomes, *Why Bad Humans?*, to which the answer is less clear. Philosophers, psychologists, theologians, doctors and sociologists, among others, continue to puzzle over it, and even to dispute whether bad humans exist any more than bad dogs. Original Sin, some say, society say others. I incline to the Original Sin side of the argument; at least Original Sin is taken as a metaphor rather than an actual historical event, a tragic flaw in our nature that leads us to demand incompatible goals in life and makes it impossible for us to reach a state of perfect peace and contentment.

By comparison with our (human) dissatisfactions, those of Ramses were slight and short-lived. He was, for example, inclined to jealousy. If my wife and I embraced, he wanted to be included. He would try to wriggle between us until one of us picked him up and cuddled him. If my wife had gone to bed before me and taken Ramses with her, so that he was already lying on the bed when I arrived, he would snarl at me slightly as I joined them; he wanted my wife to himself. (I had slight feelings of jealousy towards him myself, fearing that he loved my wife more than me, for he did not make the same scene when he and I had gone to bed first, before my wife. Perhaps Ramses was merely being chivalrous, making the distinction between the sexes among humans as well as among dogs, and felt it necessary to defend the honour of females.) Of course, he soon recovered from his fit of jealousy and was as affectionate towards me as ever.

I record the extremity of our feelings for Ramses not as they ought to have been had we been fully rational (whatever being fully rational entails), or had our situation been other than it was, but as they were.

In logic, should those feelings have changed our attitude to the whole of the animate world? After all, the very idea of someone mistreating him made our blood run cold—and hot at the same time. What of other animals?

One evening, we went to a concert in a church in a nearby town and we took Ramses with us in the car, in which we left him for the duration of the concert. We were careful to leave a window partially open for him, even though it was not particularly hot, and a little bowl of water. However, we forgot to lock the car, and when we returned, Ramses was gone. Someone must have let him out.

We had difficulty at first in believing it. We looked under the seats as if he had hidden under them to tease, or to punish, us. When it became indisputably clear to us that he was gone, we walked in the nearby streets, calling to him. We half-expected him to come running towards us when he heard us—surely he hadn't wandered far—but our calls went without response. He was lost.

He couldn't have climbed out of the window; it was beyond his reach and not open nearly wide enough for him to have done so in any case. Someone, trying the door of the car, had found it unlocked and let him out. Whoever did so was not reacting to any expression of distress by him, for he was used to being left in the car and we had observed him often settling down in these circumstances to sleep. No: the person who let Ramses out of the car was acting either from malice or from a misplaced belief that dogs should be free, as if they could and should fend for themselves in a modern English town.

I favoured the hypothesis of malignity, not only because I had seen so much of it in my work and quite possibly was prone to overestimate its prevalence and importance in human life, but because the very act of discovery that the car door was unlocked was more than likely a sign of dishonesty. The ability to cause distress to unknown others, especially without effort or likelihood of discovery, is a pleasure to some people, perhaps a compensation for a life that does not meet their hopes or expectations. Here was a case of the unmotivated malignity which Coleridge mistakenly attributed to Iago. Everyone, even the person who does not like dogs himself, knows how much people value their dogs, and how much grief their loss entails.

It is just possible that the person who let him out from the car thought that he was being kind to Ramses, or that he was protesting against the status of dogs as pets, for those who protest these days are often more attached to the purity of their motives than to the actual effects of their protests. For such a person, the suffering caused to us by learning that Ramses had, say, been run over and killed as a consequence of his 'liberation' would only be a just reward for having 'imprisoned' him as a pet in the first place. Indeed, releasing him was a kind of manumission, as the status of pet was akin to slavery. We live in times of ideological monomania.

Perhaps he had been stolen for sale to someone else. Apparently, there are dog thieves who steal to order: a Weimaraner here, a poodle there.

Fortunately, I saw that I had a message on my mobile telephone. It relieved our desperation so completely and so immediately, and was such a happiness, that it was almost worth having been desperate. A very nice lady had found Ramses wandering in the street, understood at once that he was lost, and had taken him to the nearest police station. Naturally, we rushed there as quickly as possible: it was about to close for the night, when of course most disorder and crime was likely to occur.

There was Ramses, looking miserable, but in a special facility at the station for lost dogs, far more comfortable than a police cell for arrested miscreants whether merely suspected or caught red-handed. (In the course of my work, I became more than usually acquainted with police cells.) There were baskets and blankets, as well as toys for him to play with, but these did not console him. He jumped for joy when he saw us. There could have been no better illustration of the evident fact that physical comfort, though not to be despised in itself, is not the whole of happiness.

We telephoned the lady who had found him and thanked her profusely. She had a dog herself and said that she knew how painful it would be to lose one, especially through carelessness. She knew that Ramses was loved by the trust he had in her. He was neither afraid nor aggressive. We sent her flowers.

The episode ended happily, and restored, or boosted, our faith in the possibility of human kindness. Nevertheless, when we considered how it might have ended, we experienced a kind of anticipatory grief in our imaginations.

Ever afterwards, whenever I see a poster on a lamp-post asking for information about a missing dog (or even a cat), I experience a kind of heartache. "Only an animal!" Only a person who had not known the solace of an animal's companionship would think or say such a thing.

As I have hinted, in logic, our attachment to Ramses should have affected our entire attitude to the animal world, if not the animate world. Were other animals capable of all, or some, or even more, ways of attaching humans to themselves? When a friend of mine started to keep chickens, for example, I asked her whether they ever learned to recognise her, the prerequisite of a two-way relationship. She replied that they came to her when she took food to them, but might have done the same to anyone who brought food to them: it was the act of bringing food, not the bringer of food, that they recognised. I recalled a passage from Bertrand Russell's *The Problems of Philosophy* with regard to induction, the process by which we argue from repetitions of experience to supposedly invariant laws:

> … [R]ather crude expectations of uniformity are liable to be misleading. The man who has fed the chicken every day throughout its life at last wrings its neck instead, showing that more refined views as to the uniformity of nature would have been useful to the chicken.

Still, my friend grew fond of her chickens and was sad when a fox—an urban fox, as most foxes are nowadays—got them and left nothing but feathers and bloody carcasses. Foxes are canids, close biological relatives of dogs (a Russian biologist bred foxes over several generations, selecting and interbreeding them for their most dog-like characteristics, and eventually bred foxes that resembled dogs), and one of their unpleasant characteristics is that they seem to kill for the sheer pleasure of doing so, as do leopards, and not merely for food. Absurd as it no doubt is, one cannot but feel a frisson of moral outrage at the sight of a fox-invaded chicken coop. One could accept the theft of a single chicken in the way that one can accept the theft of a sandwich by an impoverished hungry person: but to decimate an entire coop for no reason, that we cannot accept.

What hypocrites we humans are!

Our friend's chickens were rescue chickens, that is to say, egg-layers whose productivity had declined to the point at which, economically, they were no longer worth their keep and would be killed unless someone could be found to give them a home. But for the advent of the fox, they would have had three or four years of happy retirement, as did subsequent rescue chickens more carefully protected from foxes.

Rescue chickens, however, are as statistically fortunate as winners of the jackpot in lotteries—assuming, of course, that such chickens prefer to be alive than dead, or looked after rather than killed. For every chicken that is rescued, there must be a hundred million—or a very large number indeed, so large that it makes no moral difference—who are not.

And from what conditions are they rescued! I visited a battery farm (if farm is quite the word for it) nearly fifty years ago, and was appalled. It was of 'only' three thousand chickens, almost a cottage industry by today's standards, but the smell and noise, and above all the tiny wire cages in which the birds spent their entire lives, from which they became so physically inseparable that their feet, which had ankylosed round the wire-netting floor, had to be amputated while they were still living to remove them from the cages, their eggs having been taken away by conveyor belt during their productive period, made it a vision of an avian hell enclosed in a large corrugated iron shed.

The farmer was proud rather than ashamed of his enterprise, for not only was it profitable, at least for the moment (though he was probably squeezed out later by more highly capitalised and larger-scale enterprises), but he thought it was socially useful, bringing chicken to the masses. I am old enough to remember the days when chicken was a luxury food, to be looked forward to as a weekly treat, rather than rendered into nuggets, burgers, wings, thighs, and legs. In those benighted and impoverished far-off days, chickens ran about in farmers' yards in relatively small numbers, and were accordingly high-priced. Was the bringing of the meat of chickens, and of eggs, to the masses worth the aggregate of chickens' suffering?

I am not sure how to answer this question definitively. I suppose that a moral rigorist would say that if there were an alternative that could feed the masses just as well, it should be chosen. After all, Man can live without chicken nuggets, and indeed has done so for some tens of thousands of years. But I have shamefacedly to admit still to liking chicken in tarragon; roast chicken; chicken soup; chicken grilled with garlic, lime and ginger; and saag chicken.

Though my visit to the battery farm appalled me, it did not change my eating habits, as perhaps it should have done. Strictly speaking, I neither forgot nor remembered it: I put it to the back of my mind. I could always remember it if I wished, but I did not wish, because I wanted to eat my chicken in mental peace. I bought free-range chicken for preference, not only because it tasted better, but because I thought that it had had a better life before being sacrificed to my appetite—at the same time being aware that free-range is a relative term, even a term of art, and did not mean chickens raised free in the Rocky Mountains or even the Chiltern Hills. The human mind is, among other things, an instrument for avoiding unpleasant realities.

Nevertheless, our attachment to Ramses did revive in that instrument, my mind, the question of our relations with animals. How could I reasonably abominate the imagined prospect of cruelty to Ramses while condoning systematic cruelty towards animals of perhaps only a slightly lower level of mental sophistication than he, pigs for example, cruelty that I knew to be necessary to produce the food I ate at a price I could afford?

Because of Ramses, I became more sympathetic to vegetarianism, though without becoming vegetarian. We altered our diet somewhat in the direction of vegetable food, though this might also have been the effect of age, when the taste for meat, especially beef, declines. We ate much less pork. I explained, or explained away, my inconsistency by telling myself that if no one ate pork, beef, chicken or lamb, and no one consumed animal products, then pigs, cows, chickens and sheep would die out. And in the case of sheep on the Welsh hillsides, useless for other kinds of farming, would it be better for them never to have lived than never to have lived and died?

It is not difficult to find philosophers and others who oppose the keeping of pets, because it is against the dignity and rights of animals. A professor of psychology, Dr. Herzog, is of the opinion that the more we humanise animals, the less right we have to control every aspect of their lives, the logical conclusion to this being the same as that of orthodox Moslems, namely that pets *qua* pets are forbidden. Dr. Herzog, before he became a convert to his own argument, kept a pet parrot which he then released from its cage and let fly out of the window, in the full knowledge that by so doing, he was probably condemning it to death by starvation, or by cold, or by some such. Give it liberty or give it death, was his motto. Such a death was more in accordance with avian dignity, because the bird died free and autonomous. (Probably Dr. Herzog is in favour of social security, however.) This is a fine example of how a man, starting from a first principle and applying impeccable logic reaches an absurd conclusion, and prefers to act on that conclusion than to examine or refine his premise or his logic. As religion recedes and tertiary education spreads, we can expect an ever greater number of Savonarolas of their self-generated doctrine.

We cannot claim to have given Ramses a perfect life, but it was a rich and, on the whole, a happy one. He gave us happiness which I think we returned. Not much more could be demanded of a relationship.

I have written this memoir not in the hope or expectation that many will read it, though naturally I should be glad if many did, but content in the knowledge that, mouldering unread on the back shelves of some immense library, there will exist at least some slight memorial to the charming dog whom we loved, and who was of course the cleverest, friendliest, most understanding and amusing dog that ever was—who just happened to be ours. His name was Ramses.